Nov. 30/94

To a special sister
and friend!

Love,

Valerie &
Brad.

D0122470

The
FRIENDSHIP
BOOK

of Francis Gay

D. C. THOMSON & CO., LTD.
London   Glasgow   Manchester   Dundee

A Thought
For Each Day
in 1995

Love accomplishes all things.
Petrarch.

FOLLOW ME

# JANUARY

<u>SUNDAY—JANUARY 1.</u>

FOR other foundation can no man lay than that is laid, which is Jesus Christ.

Corinthians I 3:11

<u>MONDAY—JANUARY 2.</u>

A FRIEND who occasionally passes on a copy of her church magazine has marked this verse in the January issue — an appropriate thought for a new year.

Our life is a book of chapters three,
The past, the present and the yet to be.
The past is gone, it is stowed away,
The present we live with every day.
The future is not for us to see,
It is locked away and God holds the key.

The Lady of the House and I wish you a very happy New Year!

<u>TUESDAY—JANUARY 3.</u>

I HAVE just been admiring the picture on the front of an old magazine. It was of a farm labourer, in his eighties and still working with the scythe. Like his father and grandfather before him, he had spent the whole of his life on the same farm.

His work must have been hard, his hours long, and more than likely his pay low. Yet, the old man's face bore an expression of contentment.

As many of us have discovered, wealth does not necessarily make for true happiness. Real riches lie in a lifetime of love and loyalty, doing our best in whatever situation arises, and in a thankful heart.

THE FRIENDSHIP BOOK

I ALWAYS spend an hour with my two diaries at this time of year, transferring names, addresses, phone numbers, birthdays, anniversaries and details of meetings from the old diary to the snow-white pages of the new one. It's quite a task, for in the course of a year you can collect copious bits and pieces of information, some useful, some not.

It's always a job well done and later, with a murmur of satisfaction, I put the new diary in my pocket for easy reference and place the old one in my cupboard. The old year is now behind me, I am making a fresh start, and as I once read:

Trust the past to the mercy of God,
The present to His love,
And the future to His providence.

THERE is a story told about a new village policeman who was keen to get on. A number of residents were very soon reprimanded for minor offences, and the only one to escape was the vicar.

Then one night the policeman saw him coming down the hill on his bicycle and, as he approached the zebra crossing at the bottom, he stepped smartly off the pavement. The vicar jammed on his brakes and stopped just short.

"I nearly had you that time, sir," said the officer.

"Yes, Constable," replied the vicar, "but you see, the Lord was with me."

Pricking up his ears and taking out his notebook the policeman said, "I see. Two on a bike. Now that *is* an offence . . ."

It's just an amusing story, but we can still read it and smile.

THE FRIENDSHIP BOOK

AFTER a sudden and heavy snowfall our local schools were closed for a day or two. When they re-opened one of the teachers went into her classroom and said she hoped that all the children had made good use of their extra holiday. They all nodded fervently.

"What did you do while you were at home, Nicholas?" she asked.

"Oh, I prayed for more snow, Miss," he replied.

THE BBC broadcast "Songs Of Praise" from the Princess Alice Hospice in Surrey a few years ago. The programme aroused special interest among viewers, for as well as introducing patients and staff, it featured an English Setter called Levi. Along with his owner, Jan Etherington, he is a regular visitor, for Levi is a registered PAT dog, the slogan used to describe using "Pets As Therapy".

Dogs and cats have long been welcomed and recognised as valuable aids in certain types of patient care, and Levi was described by medical staff as "central to the hospice's success." The main problem seemed to be avoiding the many biscuits and chocolates being put aside for him!

Levi is just one of 5,700 dogs with the special qualities needed for hospital work — good health, friendliness, a gentle temperament. Such dogs can be guaranteed to bring friendship with wagging tails to patients in many hospices and different kinds of long-stay hospitals.

The pleasure they give can perhaps only be fully appreciated by those on the receiving end, so today I would like to give a pat on the back to all those very special therapy dogs.

THE FRIENDSHIP BOOK

THEN were there brought unto him little children, that he should put his hands on them, and pray: and the disciples rebuked them. But Jesus said, Suffer little children, and forbid them not, to come unto me: for of such is the kingdom of heaven.

Matthew 19:13-14

I NEVER fail to be impressed by how some ministers are still remembered in their parishes long after their deaths. Such a one was the Rev. John Gerard, minister of St Peter's on the Orkney island of South Ronaldsay, in the first half of last century. He is fondly remembered, not so much for his good works, but for his sense of humour and humanity.

Dogs were permitted into St Peter's during services, and he more than once stopped proceedings so that the congregation could watch a dog-fight in the aisle. "I hope the little one wins," he would say.

On one occasion he announced, "Brethren, I find the mice have been at my sermon, so I'll just begin where they left off."

He spoke to the people in simple language they understood, urging the children to let Bible truths stick to their hearts like the butter did to their bannocks at breakfast.

Another time he preached on the virtues of goodwill and tolerance, though he added, with mock sorrow, "It is impossible to live at peace with some men, for there is Willie Sinclair in the gallery, who borrowed a caisie (straw basket) from me six weeks ago and has not yet returned it!"

No wonder they say there was never a dull moment in St Peter's when John Gerard was in the pulpit!

HOW I love books! I'd feel very deprived if I woke up one morning without anything fresh to read, and I have every sympathy with the man I heard of who was reduced to reading the cornflakes packet at the breakfast table.

Books have long been a form of instruction, relaxation and recreation. In one of his essays Sir Francis Bacon wrote: "Some books are to be tasted, others to be swallowed and some few to be chewed and digested; that is, some books are to be read only in parts; others to be read, but not curiously; and some few to be read wholly and with diligence and attention." In "The Tatler", Sir Richard Steele wrote: "Reading is to the mind what exercise is to the body."

Then there are Hilaire Belloc's witty words:

When I am dead, I hope it may be said:
His sins were scarlet, but his books were read.

So here's to our favourite books and all the pleasure they have given us.

WEDNESDAY—JANUARY 11.

THE writer and preacher Henry Drummond once said: "Good acts make good men; kind acts, kind men; divine acts, divine men . . ."

In similar vein, another unknown writer commented: "Kind words are the music of the world. They have a power which seems to be beyond natural causes."

As someone else pointed out: "Kindness is a language the dumb can speak, and the deaf hear and understand."

How very true.

SNOWDROPS

THE Snowdrops bloom — and yet I know,
That born of wind and rain,
These flowers — so like the driven snow —
Are part of joy and pain.

For joy and pain have each a part,
Within our lives to play,
And smiles and tears come to the heart,
Most every passing day.

And, if perchance the pain should be
Almost too much to bear,
May some sad heart, within my life,
Find Snowdrops growing there.

Margaret Dixon.

TODAY I would like to share with you some more items from my collection of points to ponder:

One out of ten people in the world is born to aggravate the other nine.

Never do or say today things you cannot live with tomorrow.

If we listened more carefully to what is happening today, then history might not have to repeat itself so often.

Chance made us sisters — hearts made us friends.

What a big difference there is between giving advice and lending a hand.

If I can't be thankful for what I receive, I'll be thankful for what I escape.

TWO HAPPY
PEOPLE

THE FRIENDSHIP BOOK

WHEN Joan Crane was clearing out a cupboard she came across an empty flour bag dating back to 1901. She wondered if it would be of historical interest to the company which had milled the original contents so she wrote to McDougall about it. They were indeed interested and offered Joan £20 for it, but she told them that she had been a lifelong supporter of the Children's Society and asked for the money to be sent on to the society.

The firm was so impressed with her gesture that they decided to become involved themselves. As a result, in 1992 they became the sponsors of the Society's annual "Cake Bake", to the tune of £15,000.

The aim was to raise £150,000 to finance some of the work of the Children's Society — supporting children and families with problems of unemployment, disabilities, learning difficulties and so on, and in changing the conditions that stand in their way.

Jesus told a story about the mustard seed, the least of all seeds, which when it is grown is the greatest among herbs and becomes a tree so that the birds of the air can perch on its branches.

So when I think about Joan Crane and her flour bag, I am reminded that there is nothing, however small or insignificant, that is not capable of growth. I am reminded also of something my grandmother used to say, "Cast your bread upon the water and it will come back buttered."

AND the glory of the Lord shall be revealed, and all flesh shall see it together: for the mouth of the Lord hath spoken it.

Isaiah 40:5

THE FRIENDSHIP BOOK

SIR EDWARD GREY, later 1st Viscount of Fallodon, was one of the most powerful political figures of his day in the 19th and 20th centuries. Away from Westminster, however, he was a very different man.

Anyone visiting him at his country estate in Northumberland quickly realised that what mattered to him there was the assembly of wild birds in his garden. He had won the confidence of many of them so that they fed from his hand, and in the last Spring of his life was overjoyed when a robin not only sat on his outstretched hand to peck the crumbs, but then perched on top of his head to deliver a burst of song as if in thanks.

A visitor who witnessed Grey's delight declared he was more proud of that than of all his achievements as a statesman.

GOOD friends of ours have been married for 64 years, and during that time nobody ever heard a cross word pass between them.

When asked at their Diamond Wedding Anniversary to what they attributed their lifelong happiness together, Helen told us that on the day they were married they decided to outlaw the words "me" and "mine".

In their place went "we" and "ours" and they vowed that whatever life brought — joy or sorrow, riches or poverty, sickness or health — it would be "ours" to share and together "we" would tackle it.

A simple enough solution. If only more people would adopt it the world would surely be a happier place.

THE FRIENDSHIP BOOK

DURING the annual week for Christian Unity in January, our local churches get together for a Christingle service. Everyone, young and old, carries an orange with a candle inserted in it symbolising Jesus Christ The Light of the World, while round the orange is a decoration of sweets and nuts representing the fruits of the earth. With our lighted candles we form an unbroken circle inside the church.

At the beginning of the service we receive a Peace Candle as a gift from another church. The story behind it is that in 1986 a party of Christians from America visited the Soviet Union. On their departure an old lady from the Russian Orthodox Church gave the minister three roubles, and asked him to buy a candle and take it back to his church in Pennsylvania as a gesture of goodwill.

The idea spread amongst other churches in the USA, and somehow or other a candle arrived in the UK at a church in Sutton Coldfield. From there the practice of giving candles spread between churches here.

So one more Peace Candle was lit, the symbol of our hope for the peace and unity of the whole world, for as it was said, there is not so much darkness that one small candle cannot overcome it:

"I shall light a candle of understanding in thine heart, which shall not be put out."

Esdras II: The Apocrypha.

RICHARD JEFFRIES is the author of these apt lines:

"The hours when the mind is absorbed by beauty are the only hours we live."

THE FRIENDSHIP BOOK

"HOW do you like my new calendar, Francis?" asked our friend Mary as we sat at her fire enjoying a cup of tea. We agreed it was attractive and she continued:

"It's from my friend Doris who went to live with her daughter in Australia. It didn't arrive until well into January, but it has given me so much pleasure. You see, all our Winter months are their Summer ones, and so the pictures are of lovely outdoor scenes — parks and flowers, surfing and picnics and children paddling. I keep it on the wall here, just by my armchair, and if the weather outside looks cold and miserable, well, I just turn my back on it and think about Doris enjoying all that lovely sunshine."

With such a serene and positive outlook, it's no wonder we come away from Mary's house feeling all the better for having spent an hour with her!

A BURMESE potter had become envious of the prosperity of a washerman. Determined to put this man out of business, the potter persuaded the king to issue an order requiring the man to wash one of the emperor's black elephants and make it white.

The washerman replied that according to the rules of his vocation he would need a vessel large enough to hold the elephant, whereupon the king commanded the potter to provide one. So the potter constructed a giant bowl and had it carefully delivered.

When the elephant stepped into it, the structure cracked beneath the weight of the enormous beast. Many more vessels were made, but each was crushed in the same way. Eventually it was the potter who was put out of business by the very scheme he had devised to ruin the man he envied.

THE FRIENDSHIP BOOK

THE Lord our God be with us, as he was with our fathers; let him not leave us, nor forsake us: That he may incline our hearts unto him, to walk in all his ways, and to keep his commandments, and his statutes, and his judgments, which he commanded our fathers.

Kings I 8:57-58

WHEN Jim's wife Louise died, he was very low. They'd been a close couple and some folk thought he wouldn't get over it. He took to revisiting all the places she had loved and where she had been happy.

One day he turned up at an old shop in which she had worked as a girl when they had first met and fallen in love. She had been a dressmaker there, and now he asked the proprietor if he could see the little room in which she'd spent her working hours. She had often told him about it, but he had never seen it.

The proprietor hesitated and then led Jim up a rickety stair to the room, no longer in use. Jim gazed inside, imagining her sitting there in her fresh young beauty. Suddenly his eye caught some words scratched on the wall behind where she had sat. He went closer and read "Louise Loves Jim Very Much". Quietly, the proprietor explained that Louise had written it herself years ago.

You might think that Jim would be sadder than ever after that, but somehow it helped to pull him through. That simple message from years ago gave him comfort and the strength he needed to carry on, secure in the knowledge that Louise's love, in a mysterious way, surrounded him still.

THE FRIENDSHIP BOOK

WHEN days are at their coldest and dreariest, when we can hardly see across the street because of the fog, and when the branches of trees are heavily frosted, the Lady of the House likes to begin what she calls her "cheerful game".

She is on the lookout for all the things that give her particular pleasure and she makes a note of them in her diary — the appearance of clusters of Christmas roses in the garden; the passing of the shortest day and evidence that daylight is gradually getting longer and stronger; the first snowdrop; the day that the bowl of pink hyacinths in our sitting-room fills the air with its perfume; the first occasion we are able to have tea without the light on; buds on the beech trees; carpets of crocuses; the first night she is able to go to bed without her hot-water bottle.

The list appears to be endless, for as my wife remarked, "You know, Francis, the more I practise the cheerful game, the more things I find to be thankful about."

I'm sure we could all feel the benefit of playing that game.

MEETING POINT

WHEN someone is lonely
  Perhaps in your street,
Why not brighten tomorrow
  By arranging to meet?
And you'll bring contentment
  To that person's day,
By starting a friendship
  In the friendliest way!

Elizabeth Gozney.

THE FRIENDSHIP BOOK

I HAVE a friend who says he divides people into taps and drains. The taps are those who are always ready and waiting to help. You have just to reach out and they will pour out comfort, good cheer and clear commonsense in a steady, refreshing stream. Their kindness never runs dry.

And the drains? They are the ones who disappear when you need them. They have nothing to give, but only take. Whatever you offer them, it's gone in a flash and never a word of thanks.

Don't you hope that my friend would think of you as a tap? I certainly pray that I'm one. I would hate to be a drain!

OUR house was buffeted by a gale recently and I began to think of the many ways in which the word wind is used in our language.

We speak about an "ill wind" that is likely to bring mishaps or misfortune in its wake. If someone is taking risks in business or legal matters, we say that he is "sailing close to the wind". If we have a suspicion of a scheme being secretly planned, we smile to ourselves and say, "So that's the way the wind blows".

An eminent politician coined the phrase that a "wind of change" was blowing across a country. A visit to the dentist or the anticipation of a driving test can cause us to "get the wind up". On a lighter note a "whirlwind romance" is usually a very ardent and short courtship before marriage.

The most wonderful and exciting wind known to Christians everywhere was the "rushing mighty wind". It aptly described the coming of the Holy Spirit at Pentecost.

THE FRIENDSHIP BOOK

I WONDER if you have ever watched "The Golden Girls", the American television comedy? It featured four ladies in the older age group who lived together, found companionship together, and had their ups and downs, but whatever happened would stand by each other.

Some time ago I watched a programme about some real-life "Golden Girls" from Chorley in Lancashire who had discovered the joy of supportive female friendship. Norah, Rose, Wynne and Dorothy were all widows, living alone, but they were relishing their golden years, drawing spirit and energy from each other. Together they shopped for new clothes, swam, danced, went to French classes and helped one another to cope with loneliness.

Amongst the insights they shared were, "Golden days are calmer, it's how in tune you are with them. They bring independence and freedom. They are the beginning of the rest of my life." "Some friends get off along the way to keep various pressing appointments. A few stay with you to the very end." "Put on a smile. It not only makes you look nicer, but makes a nicer sound."

The positive message of those four real-life "Golden Girls" was that, whatever we may have heard to the contrary, growing older can not only be rewarding, but beneficial, too.

TRUST in the Lord with all thine heart; and lean not unto thine own understanding. In all thy ways acknowledge him, and he shall direct thy paths.

Proverbs 3:56

THE FRIENDSHIP BOOK

MONDAY—JANUARY 30.

AFTER 42 years Margaret Phillips of Dundee gave up smoking.

"How did you manage it?" I asked when I congratulated her. I knew she had tried before and failed.

"It was so easy," she beamed. "I decided I would stop on my mother's birthday. She died a long time ago, but it's always been a very special day for me."

"So that helped you?" I said.

"Oh, yes, Francis. You see, I vowed never to touch another cigarette from that day on. I would be letting my mother down if I broke that vow, wouldn't I? I know she had faith in me."

So, long after she passed on, Margaret's mother has transformed her daughter's life. Her guiding hand is still there. I think that's rather wonderful, don't you?

TUESDAY—JANUARY 31.

IT can be quite heartening to learn that many great men have had to learn to overcome their deficiencies and are not so different from the rest of us, after all.

George Bernard Shaw was so painfully shy that he would sometimes walk up and down the street for up to 20 minutes before he could summon courage to knock on somebody's door.

When he was asked how he managed to speak in public in spite of such timidity, his reply was, "The same way I learned to skate — by doggedly making a fool of myself until I got used to it."

As the old proverb so aptly says, "If at first you don't succeed, try, try again."

FEBRUARY

I RECEIVED a letter one day from another Lady of the House whose leg had been in plaster since she fell on a patch of ice. She was full of praise for the way her husband had looked after her.

"He's done all the shopping, cooking and a hundred and one things to keep me from fretting about the housework. When I shed bits from my plaster cast, he's never far behind with the carpet sweeper. He really does deserve a gold medal."

So today I raise my glass to all those "gold medallists" — of both sexes — who hold the fort so heroically while their other half is indisposed. Bless them all!

FRED isn't getting any younger, and lately he has become rather deaf, which makes him feel somewhat depressed.

One day, however, he came across something written by Thomas Alva Edison, the developer of the light bulb, who had suffered from the same problem.

"This deafness has been a great advantage to me in many ways. When in a telegraph office I could hear only the instrument on the table at which I sat and, unlike the other operators in the room, I was not distracted by the other instruments. Another very great advantage is that I have been enabled to preserve my nerves intact. Broadway is as quiet to me as a country village is to a person with normal hearing."

So maybe being hard of hearing has some advantages, after all!

RICHES

I USED *to wish and plan and dream,*
  And think of things I'd like to do.
So many things I longed to buy,
  But now I'm older, wiser, too.

What do I need, but hearth and home,
  Enough to eat, a bed, a chair?
And gifts that money cannot buy,
  A friend to keep and love to share?

The years have flown so quickly by,
  And I see life another way.
Just like the miser counts his gold,
  I count my riches every day!

Iris Hesselden.

MY imagination was stimulated by the following line from a church publication:—

"A closed hand cannot receive."

How true! Have you ever thought of the many things you cannot do if your hand is closed?

You can't shake hands. You can't wave a friendly greeting (only shake a fist), you can't pat a child on the head or place a reassuring hand on the shoulder of someone who is discouraged. You can't stroke a beloved pet. You can't turn the pages of a book or play a musical instrument. You can't plant seeds or pick a flower.

Let us be thankful for the joys that come to us through our own open hands and those of others.

CRISP AND EVEN

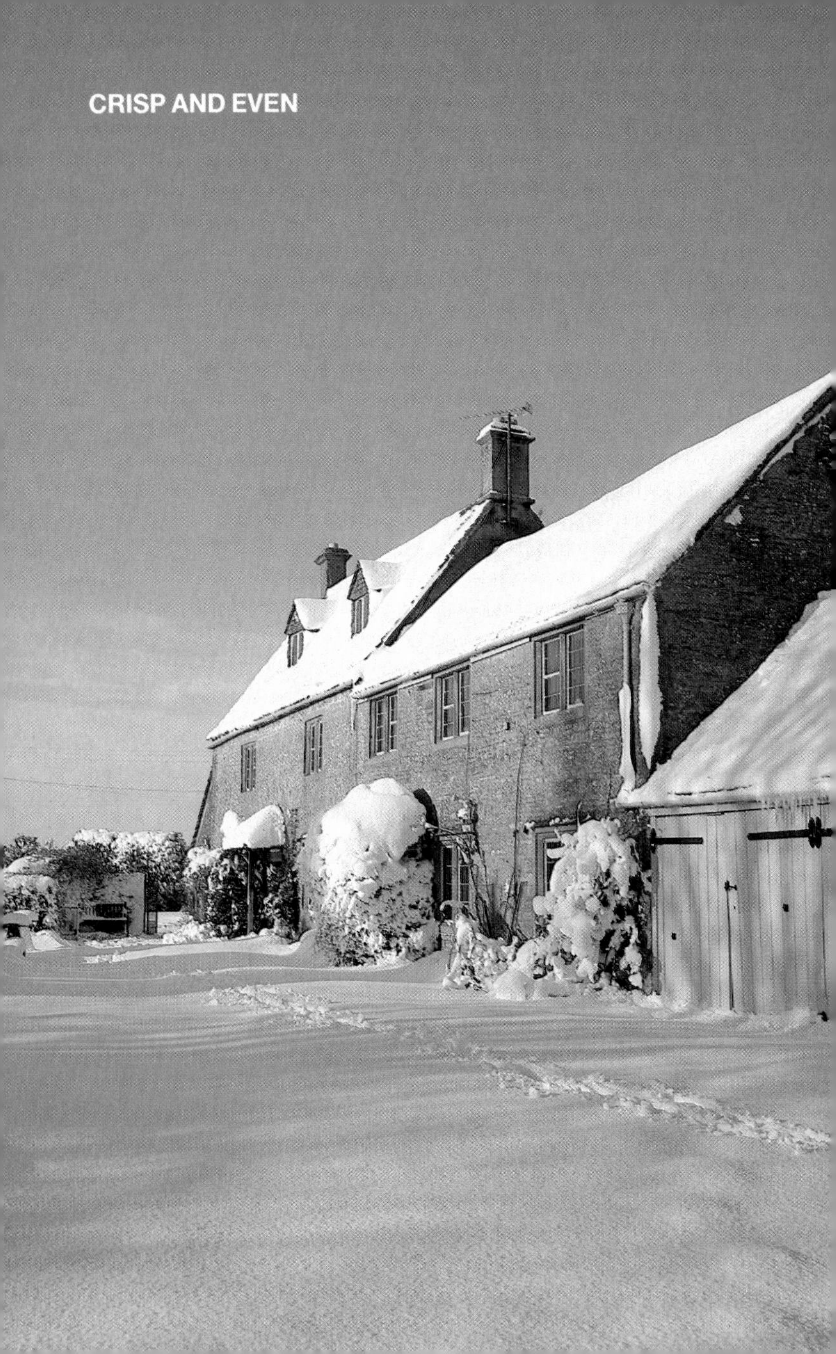

THE FRIENDSHIP BOOK

BEWARE lest any man spoil you through philosophy and vain deceit, after the tradition of men, after the rudiments of the world, and not after Christ.

Colossians 2:8

THERE'S nothing like feeling at home with the people with whom you have to work. It makes for a happier, more relaxed environment.

A Yorkshire teacher had just started work in a junior school when she fell and damaged two front teeth. The dentist had to remove them, and told her she might have to wait a week or two for crowns to be fitted. What a handicap, she thought, but the headmistress reassured her.

"It will help you a lot. When you start work in the morning just notice how many of the children have front teeth missing. They will feel you are one of them!"

Quite a price to pay for popularity, though!

THE Tate family join everything. Then Ro Tate tries to change it all. Agi Tate stirs up trouble, and Irri Tate helps him. If something new is suggested Hesi Tate and Vege Tate throw cold water on the idea.

Imi Tate tries to mimic everyone. Devas Tate is thoroughly disruptive, and Poten Tate wants to be so important. Facili Tate, Medi Tate and Cogi Tate together get things right.

How true!

THE FRIENDSHIP BOOK

DO you ever wonder why some of us appear to be so plain and ordinary while others seem striking in comparison? "It isn't fair," we grumble, glaring into the mirror balefully.

Take heart, though, and remember the old gardener whose plot was a glorious riot of colour and beauty, except for one small patch of the original old stock of polyanthus — plain and somewhat drab.

"Why do you keep those when there are so many brightly-coloured modern plants to choose from?" he was asked.

"Ah, but the plain ones set off the rest," he replied.

It's true, isn't it? We and our talents may not be showy, but we all have our special purpose in life.

PERHAPS it is wrong of me but I can feel a certain reluctant regard and admiration for poachers. Maybe the old "Lincolnshire Poacher's Song" we learned at school makes them sound like likeable rogues, rather than out-and-out wrongdoers.

I like a story I read in a Yorkshire paper about an old Dales village poacher who was seriously ill. One day his enemy, the local gamekeeper, called to see him.

Almost at his last gasp, the poacher agreed to be reconciled with the gamekeeper, and there was a touching scene as the two shook hands and called an end to their old feud. The gamekeeper, quite overcome, was about to leave in tears, but at the door he was called back and the old poacher gasped, "But think on, Fred, if I should happen to get better, all this is off!"

There was life in the old dog yet!

THE FRIENDSHIP BOOK

TODAY, I'd like to share "lots" with you.

Care a lot,
  And share a lot,
    But never court despair a lot.

Strive a lot,
  And thrive a lot,
    By keeping hopes alive a lot.

Befriend a lot,
  And mend a lot
    Of bridges we can tend a lot.

Try a lot,
  Apply a lot
    Of never saying die a lot.

I HAVE been reading what some famous men have said about coping with the difficulties of life.

General Charles de Gaulle said, "I find difficulties and problems attractive. It is only by coming to grips with difficulty that I can realise my potentialities": while Bishop Philip Brooks wrote, "I do not pray for an easy life, I pray to be a stronger man; I do not pray for tasks equal to my powers, but pray for powers equal to my tasks."

John Mason Neale, remembered for his carols "Good King Wenceslas" and "Good Christian Men Rejoice", is quoted as saying, "If possible it shall be done, and if impossible it *must* be done."

Most of all, though, I like the heartfelt prayer of an unknown writer, "Lord, when I get to the end of my tether, tie a knot for me to hold on to!"

THE FRIENDSHIP BOOK

THE Lord by wisdom hath founded the earth; by understanding hath he established the heavens.

Proverbs 3:19

PERHAPS the restaurant owner who placed this notice in his window didn't attract many new customers, but he certainly caused a lot of amusement:

TRY ONE OF OUR MEALS —
YOU'LL NEVER GET BETTER!

THE pansy is perhaps one of our favourite cottage garden flowers. With its gorgeous colours and the faces we imagine we can see, it's as if we greet a row of friends every time we stroll along the path.

"And there is pansies, that's for thoughts," said Shakespeare's Ophelia, for it is the emblem of love and kind thoughts. It is therefore a flower particularly associated with St Valentine's Day. In years gone by it was believed that an infusion of its leaves would cure a broken heart.

Pansies are known by a number of other names such as Heartsease, Two-faces-under-the-sun and Face-and-hood. Sometimes they are called Herb Trinity, for they often have three colours and three petals to remind us of the Holy Trinity.

In flower language the pansy symbolises contentment, so the next time I see a border of pansies, I shall try to remember all the lovely thoughts associated with them.

THE FRIENDSHIP BOOK

SAMUEL JOHNSON was one of the great characters of English literature, and among his friends was a younger man named Oliver Goldsmith.

Goldsmith was in lodgings, and wasn't a very wealthy man. When he fell behind with his rent, his landlady had him arrested.

Goldsmith requested Johnson to visit him in jail, and there asked the older man if there was anything he could do to help. He also showed Johnson a manuscript which he had written. Johnson took it, read it, then handed it straight to a London bookseller who paid him £60 for it — 230 years ago that was, of course, a considerable sum.

Not only did Goldsmith clear his debts, but that manuscript was the famous novel for which he is now especially remembered — the classic "Vicar Of Wakefield".

WALKING out one somewhat gloomy day recently, I met a friend who immediately greeted me with the cheery words, "Hello, I was thinking of you this morning." Suddenly the day wasn't gloomy any more, it had quite a rosy glow. Someone had been thinking about me.

It made me ponder — wouldn't it be nice if we could all just stop for a minute once a day, and think about someone else other than our own little mundane selves?

Only a minute . . . It doesn't sound much — but if we all did this, there's no knowing what it might achieve. We've been given so many minutes each day; surely we can spare one to be quiet and think peaceful, loving thoughts of others.

Here's my challenge — a minute a day for others.

THE FRIENDSHIP BOOK

ISN'T it wonderful how some occupations endure through the centuries? I am thinking of one, in particular — the shepherd.

We have a friend who manages a very large flock of sheep. One wet and windy evening, we were visiting his home when a motorist called with a message that a couple of sheep had been seen wandering along the road nearby. Peter quickly excused himself and went out into the rain.

It was some time later when he returned, soaked to the skin and extremely cold. The Lady of the House and I asked if he had found the stray sheep. He gave a smile of satisfaction and told us that they were now safely back in the field where they belonged.

For us that night the story of the Good Shepherd and his flock came vividly to life.

ON my way to the newsagent's, I pass a house that saddens me. The part that I can see appears clean and well-kept, but it stands behind a tall hedge and a tightly-closed gate that suggests the owner has pulled up the drawbridge and withdrawn from the world.

What a lot of happy events that owner will miss — a new baby having its first airing on a sunny day, a group of children chatting excitedly on their way home from school, a neighbour popping his head round the gate to ask how we manage to have such a fine display of roses.

If we keep ourselves too much to ourselves, we are in danger of missing many joyful moments. As the children's author Alison Uttley so aptly put it, "The world is full of diamonds if we look for them."

THE FRIENDSHIP BOOK

NOW unto God and our Father be glory for ever and ever. Amen.

Philippians 4:20

SLEEP

SUCH pleasure to be sleeping
In a cosy bed,
Tucked beneath the covers,
A pillow at my head.

Forgetting all the worries
And duties of the day,
Relaxed in blissful slumber
To sleep the night away.

Sleep, the blessed healer
Of tiredness and pain,
Wraps us in oblivion
To refresh us once again.
Dorothy M. Loughran.

THE Lady of the House invited a friend round for coffee.

"There's one thing about this house," remarked Dorothy thoughtfully. "If I put something down, it doesn't look out of place."

The Lady of the House is still trying to work out whether or not that was a compliment!

THE FRIENDSHIP BOOK

PHRENOLOGISTS claim that they can tell what type of person you are, or will be, by the bumps on your skull. Graphologists claim they can read your character through your handwriting. Physiognomists claim that they can read your character by the shape of your nose, the set of your jaw, the texture of your skin.

These are complicated ways of judging a person's character, but I'd like to tell you a quicker method. Find out the consuming passion of a person's life, their greatest love. Is it the love of money? Then no matter what the subject of the conversation, it will come back to money matters again and again. Or is it love of gossip? Then it will show on the face, and the eyes will sparkle at some spicy comment made about another. I could go on, for everyone takes on something of the countenance of the thing they love most.

That is why Faith is so important — get to know and love the Founder, and that joy will shine through, no matter how we are being assessed.

HERE is something we can all afford to give — because it won't cost a penny, and what's more we'll be the richer for having given it. Not only that, but it cuts across all language and race barriers, has no age limits, and is the shortest distance between two people. Sounds too good to be true, doesn't it? So what is it? Why, a smile, of course!

Just try it — don't wait for someone to smile at you first, take the initiative and put a little warmth into someone else's life. You'll feel warmth in return, for that is just how it works:

"Wear a smile. One size fits all."

RECENTLY, a new bridge was built over our river, by-passing the congested town centre. We should thank God for bridge builders! Just think of the complicated and lengthy journeys we'd have to make without them. We do take them for granted, all the same, rather like the people who help us through life — our family and friends, schoolteachers, club leaders, those we meet every day at work, in the shops, our neighbours. All these people influence us, and can make life pleasant and fulfilling by a word of encouragement, or a helping hand. They are the "bridge builders" of life.

Come to think of it, I'm a neighbour, a shopper, a parent and — I hope — a friend. Yes, I'm a bridge builder, too, and so are *you.*

WHEN I called to see my old friend Mary I found her in a great deal of discomfort, for she had fallen awkwardly down a short flight of stairs. No bones were broken, but she had twisted her knee badly and had been unable to put any weight on it for more than a fortnight. Yet Mary was her usual cheerful self and was determined not to let the mishap get her down.

"You know, Francis," she said, "it may seem a funny thing to say, but I know now what a footballer feels like when he has a muscle injury."

I confess I had to hide a smile, for anyone less like a footballer than Mary, I can hardly imagine. However, what a lovely quality it is when we are able to enter into another person's problems and suffering with understanding and sympathy — even when it is something outside our own experience.

THE FRIENDSHIP BOOK

BEAR ye one another's burdens, and so fulfil the law of Christ.

Galatians 6:2

HAVE you heard this old proverb?

He that knows not, and knows not, that he knows not, is a fool. Shun him.

He that knows not, and knows that he knows not, is a child. Teach him.

He that knows, and knows not that he knows, is asleep. Wake him.

He that knows, and knows that he knows, is a wise man. Follow him.

Few words, but a big message!

I FEEL sympathy for the children of ministers. I often think they must be expected to live up to high standards so difficult to achieve.

I like the story of John, a minister's son, who was called in from playing one day to join in a meal at which visitors were being entertained. His mother dispatched him immediately to wash his hands. "You know what I keep saying about germs, Johnnie," she said.

From outside the dining-room door, a little voice was clearly heard to mutter, "Germs and Jesus, it's all I hear about in this house, and I've never seen either."

No doubt in the end he would be quite convinced of their existence!

 # MARCH

I LIKE to look at everything —
A snow-capped peak, a sign of Spring;
A moonlit night, a sunny day,
A swallow winging on its way;
A rose in bloom, a cherry tree,
A shore's liaison with the sea;
A lazy river winding by
On which reflections catch the eye.
I like to look at things each day,
It's all a Theme Park in a way.
The only difference seems to be,
In Nature's park, admission's free.

                J. M. Robertson.

RECENTLY I spotted a truly thought-provoking message on a Wayside Pulpit: "You never get a second chance to make a first impression."

How true! I thought of the many times I've jumped to a conclusion about something, made a judgment of a place or person simply on the first impression. If I do this to others, then surely they must do the same!

Only yesterday an acquaintance said to me, reproachfully, "I thought I'd done something to offend you — you didn't smile as you went by!"

A promising friendship could have been nipped in the bud if Peter hadn't spoken — I'd been so busy with my own thoughts, I just hadn't seen him! It's so easy to go by first impressions, and we rarely get a second chance to put things right.

THE FRIENDSHIP BOOK

I ONCE spent a few weeks at a friend's home in the peaceful Borders countryside. Jim was a very keen Sunday School teacher and youth worker, and often talked enthusiastically about the youngsters and how he was able to help them.

A field rose steeply at the back of the house, and one morning a flock of sheep appeared in it. A few days later, Jim called me to the window. He pointed out how the sheep had already made paths for themselves by always following the same routes on the steep slope.

"They quickly found the best way across the face of the slope and up to the top," he said, "and now they always follow the same route. It's the same with my youngsters. If I can show them the best way to live now, while they're still learning, there's a very good chance they will stick to that for the rest of their lives."

When I am out walking in the hills and come on a well-worn sheep track, I often remember Jim's words as I gladly follow the path to the top.

MOST of us enjoy an occasional party. Not so Thomas Alva Edison, the great inventor, who hated all formal occasions.

At one get-together he found himself surrounded by people with whom he had absolutely nothing in common and so he decided to make an unobtrusive exit as soon as possible. However, as he edged towards the door he bumped into his host who hailed him enthusiastically, "I'm so glad you were able to come, Mr Edison. Tell me, what are you working on now?"

"My exit!" replied the inventor, truthfully.

A most inventive reply!

SUNDAY—MARCH 5.

A ND without controversy great is the mystery of godliness: God was manifest in the flesh, justified in the Spirit, seen of angels, preached unto the Gentiles, believed on in the world, received up into glory.

Timothy I 3:16

MONDAY—MARCH 6.

A WISE man once wrote that the hardest of all words any man, woman or child can say are: "Yes, I made a mistake. It's all my fault."

It is so much easier to blame someone else, or to say, "I couldn't help it!"

Once, after a great battle, Frederick the Great wrote home: "I have just lost a battle, and it's my own fault."

Perhaps, though the soldier did not know it, this confession made him a greater man than all his victories in the field ever could.

TUESDAY—MARCH 7.

H ERE are a few more thoughts from my collection of split-second sermons which may have a special message for you today:

Life's sweetest things are the quiet things.

A happy life consists in tranquillity of mind.

(Cicero)

The weariest night, the longest day, sooner or later must perforce come to an end.

(Baroness Orczy)

THE FRIENDSHIP BOOK

THE Lady of the House came home from a country walk carrying a bunch of pussy willows, those lovely slender twigs with the soft, grey buds.

As she arranged them in a vase, she asked me, "Francis, do you know how the very first ones are supposed to have come about?"

I confessed I did not.

She told me that, according to legend, a cat once gave birth to several unwanted kittens. Its owner threw them into a river. As they floated off, the cat ran along the bank mewing so plaintively that the willow trees bending over the water took pity and leaned down their branches even lower so that the kittens could climb to safety. Ever since, we have had these beautiful pussy willows every Spring.

A tall story? Of course — but I have to admit that when I stroked one of the grey buds it did feel just like a cat's fur!

DID you know that happy folk recover from illness much more readily than people who are depressed and always complaining?

The old sages always used to say that laughter was the best medicine — indeed, better than medicine.

Someone else remarked that "a merry heart does good, like medicine" — and infectious laughter is often catching. Don't you find it so? I like the anonymous verse which sums it all up:

When wholesome laughter fills the air,
Some ills will soon depart;
For laughter is good medicine
That helps to cheer the heart.

THE FRIENDSHIP BOOK

WE all have a burden to bear at some time or another and it often proves to be heavier than it should be, because we are too proud to share it.

Our young neighbour William hated mathematics. We had known that something was wrong when he started to saunter unhappily to school, and he eventually told his parents about his difficulties. They went to his teacher to explain how ill at ease he felt about the subject, and things were soon sorted out. Now we see him running happily to school again — his trouble had been shared, and thereby tackled.

So, whenever we have something on our mind, we should try to share our worries. Never forget that there is always Someone who has time and patience to listen and help.

I WONDER how often you have bought new furniture, carpets, curtains or kitchen equipment and then wondered how to dispose of the old items that still have quite a lot of life left in them?

It was in response to this situation that The Carpenters' Shop was opened in the town of Walsall, Staffordshire. Run by a team of church volunteers, they will collect any surplus, good-quality items and store them until they can be redistributed to the people who are needing those particular things.

Many have been helped through the scheme, including single parents, disabled people and the elderly, and those who have lost all their household possessions through a disaster such as a house fire.

It's an admirable project, and it is worth finding out if a similar one operates in your own locality. Participation costs the donor nothing and can make such a difference to others.

THE FRIENDSHIP BOOK

I CAN do all things through Christ which strengtheneth me.

Philippians 4:13

EARLY BIRDS

OH, do be quiet, I mutter,
As I listen to their song,
It surely can't be morning,
They must have got it wrong.
It doesn't seem five minutes,
Since I lay down to sleep,
Now these early birds a-wormin',
Rouse me with their noisy cheep.
Then when I'm fully wakened,
With my senses all in place,
I thank God for the pleasure,
Of this early morning grace.

Phyllis Ellison.

I HEARD this amusing tale recently and would like to share it with you today.

A man, sitting outside a Yorkshire Dales village inn, was surprised to see three fine cows coming round the corner driven by a working dog. Behind them followed the farmer, sitting in a Land-Rover. The onlooker was sufficiently surprised to exclaim, "I've seen everything now!"

The farmer heard this remark and called back, "Aye, idleness is wasted effort if it isn't carried out efficiently!"

THE FRIENDSHIP BOOK

AT a recent jumble sale the Lady of the House bought a dress for £1. When she arrived home she found a neatly-folded note in the pocket. It read: "Don't wash this dress with your whites — the colour runs!"

She was amazed that anybody should bother to write such a message in a garment intended for a jumble sale, but it really made her day. She wished that she had given more than a pound for the dress. It would have been worth it to acknowledge such a kindly, personal touch!

THERE was once a fisherman who also liked to play the flute. One day he set off for the seashore with his nets and settled down on a rocky ledge. There he took out his flute and began to play, thinking that the fish would be so attracted by the sound of his music that they would swim into his net.

However, he was disappointed. Although he played and played most beautifully, he caught not a single fish. In disgust he put aside the flute, cast his net into the deep water and was rewarded with a splendid catch.

It's an illustration of the wisdom of knowing the right way and the right time to do something, and then putting it into practice. As the Book of Ecclesiastes phrases it:

To everything there is a season, and a time to every season under the heaven:

A time to get, and a time to lose; a time to keep, and a time to cast away.

A time to rend, and a time to sew; a time to keep silence, and a time to speak.

THE FRIENDSHIP BOOK

ELSIE had a good job which she loved and a busy, fulfilling life — but then her husband was found to be terminally ill and she had to give up her work to look after him. She never complained, but there were times when she felt so desperate in her lonely situation, wondering if anyone cared or understood her plight.

Then a surprise arrived at the house one morning — a basket of flowers from her colleagues at work, tastefully arranged, with an encouraging message: *Thinking of you so much.* Elsie's husband could still enjoy the sight and smell of the beautiful flowers.

When Elsie phoned to tell me about the surprise, she said, "You know, it mattered *so* much to know that others were thinking of me when I needed their help most."

A token of affection that cost each workmate only a little, yet it meant so much!

HAVE you heard the story about the young man who took his wife out for a special meal on their wedding anniversary?

It was a lovely restaurant with good food, soft lights and sweet music. As the accordionist played romantic tunes, he moved from table to table until he stopped by the young couple. Picking up a red carnation he presented it to the girl with a flourish and softly whispered something in her ear.

Slightly put out, her husband said, "What did he say to you?"

"Oh," she giggled, "he asked me if I was enjoying the meringue!"

WATER COLOURS

THE FRIENDSHIP BOOK

WHEN Christ, who is our life, shall appear, then shall ye also appear with him in glory.

Colossians 3:4

HAS it ever struck you that the only calling which you can follow empty-handed is that of the ministry or priesthood?

Every tradesman needs his tools, be he plumber or carpenter, builder or glazier. The artist must have a brush, the sculptor a hammer. In the professions, the doctor and dentist have their instruments, the lawyers their papers. Even the writer must have a pen, a typewriter or a word-processor.

All that ministers require is the Word of God and love.

Of course they will often carry a Bible, but some of the greatest Christian work has been done by men and women in captivity, in prison camps or in police states where religion is forbidden.

In such conditions the Christian who has "nothing" has everything.

I CAME upon these four curious lines by the poet George Ellis born in 1753. I wonder if you can guess what he is describing:

Snowy, Flowy, Blowy,
Showery, Flowery, Bowery,
Hoppy, Croppy, Droppy,
Breezy, Sneezy, Freezy.

Yes, he was describing the 12 months of the year. They haven't changed much in 242 years, have they?

THE FRIENDSHIP BOOK

OUR friend Mary came back from an early Spring holiday with an interesting tale to tell.

While visiting a tropical bird-house, she had been absolutely entranced by a hummingbird building its nest. Living in a confined space, its only source of materials was the clothes worn by visitors.

Mary was quite literally "tickled-pink", as that day she was wearing an angora-wool pink hat, just the right thing for a warm and comfortable nest. The brightly-coloured hummingbird swooped time and time again for a tuft from her hat, to weave into the nest he was building.

Mary finished her story, saying, "God is the great provider, but I was glad on this occasion to be able to lend him a hand, or should I say a hat!"

HOW would you define happiness?

Pastor Charles is an inner-city missionary, and one day he visited a home where an unusual definition was pinned up on a wall. It read: "Happiness is an unexpected hug."

Happiness is more than that, however, and an unknown writer has three suggestions for achieving that desirable state:

Make a habit of doing something for somebody every day.

Look for something cheerful every day — a flower, a bright thought, or a good word.

Add something to remember — a motto, a verse, or a short phrase.

The writer suggests that some days these memorised thoughts will return like whispers of peace from God.

THE FRIENDSHIP BOOK

I DON'T know anything about the 19th-century Australian poet Adam Lindsay Gordon, but he deserves to be remembered for these four wise lines:

Life is mostly froth and bubble,
Two things stand like stone,
Kindness in another's trouble,
Courage in your own.

TOMORROW, the fourth Sunday in Lent, is Mothering Sunday. For at least three centuries it has been an occasion for family reunions. Its roots go back to before the Reformation when families went together to worship at their parish church.

Later, when it was the practice for boys and girls to leave their homes and serve as apprentices, they were always given a holiday on Mothering Sunday so that they could visit their mothers, taking gifts of wild flowers gathered on the waysides and made into posies. On that day, the rigid Lenten rules of eating were relaxed and the family enjoyed a special meal, with perhaps a fruity simnel cake for tea. In France the cakes were impressed with the figure of Christ or the Virgin Mary and they were known as "bread of our Lord".

Today, as in years past, it is still Mother's special day, and it is nice that families still like, whenever possible, to return home to express their gratitude for her love and care.

I like this very human prayer written by a mother:

"Teach me, Lord, to invest time and energy into the little ones entrusted to my care, that they may see you through me, however tired or drained I may feel. And please — give me patience . . ."

THE FRIENDSHIP BOOK

NOW therefore ye are no more strangers and foreigners, but fellow citizens with the saints, and of the household of God.

Ephesians 2:19

GROWING old? Well, take heart, and when you begin to feel a stick would be a help along the way, remember this remark made to me by an elderly neighbour just recently.

"I find," she said, "that with the passing years my pace gets a bit slower. It's true that I don't go as fast, or as far, but I *see* a darn sight more along the road!"

FATE had given Les a real buffeting. One of his family caused him considerable worry, his wife had a serious illness, and he had numerous business problems. He kept smiling, though, and I have seen him singing cheerfully to himself as he set off to face yet another difficult day.

One windy morning I came on him standing on the pavement gazing up into the air. When he saw me, he pointed upwards and shouted against the noise of the gale: "See the storm-cock?"

I craned my neck and saw a mistle thrush on the top of a tall tree, swaying in the wind and singing its heart out.

"The worse the storm, the louder he sings," said Les. "I reckon if he can do it, so can I!"

Blessed indeed are those who sing through life's storms. I have no worries about Les. He will survive his spell of bad luck and come out on top, singing — like the storm-cock.

BRIGHT AND BEAUTIFUL

THE FRIENDSHIP BOOK

THREE LITTLE WORDS

L OVE is so exciting,
When you're very young,
The words "I Love You" special,
When said in any tongue.
And even when your youth is spent,
And you are growing old,
If someone says "I love you",
That's worth far more than gold.

Phyllis Ellison.

D O you wear bifocal spectacles?
I know that some of you do, and indeed they are useful, because they save the bother of changing from one pair of glasses for distance to another pair for close-up activities such as reading.

My friend George was grumbling about his bifocals recently. He said that he had taken a long time to get used to wearing them, but admitted he now found them beneficial.

To have a bifocal view on life is very necessary. If we just looked on one level all the time, we would miss the close-up beauty of a ladybird on a leaf, or the sight of a rainbow on the horizon.

Y OU may well have heard this Highland farewell before, but I have always thought how encouraging it is in its winsomeness:

"Now, it would be a fine thing if you were coming instead of going."

 APRIL

I HAD been promising myself a long walk, but as I opened the door I saw large drops of rain on the ground. Next moment, it began to pour, and soon the pavements were wet and large puddles had started to form.

Disappointed, I went back inside and stared through the window. As I watched, I saw a small boy and his mother emerging from a house farther down the road. On the boy's feet were shiny red wellington boots, and on his face a smile so broad that it was obvious he regarded walking in the rain as a real treat.

Watching him happily splashing along, it occurred to me that it was a very long time indeed since I had regarded walking in the rain as an enjoyable activity. Not long afterwards, armed with umbrella and raincoat, I set off, too. I really enjoyed that walk!

What a difference a change of attitude can make to circumstances we cannot alter.

SUNDAY—APRIL 2.

I F we live in the Spirit, let us also walk in the Spirit.

Galatians 5:25

MONDAY—APRIL 3.

I WAS delighted to come on this little prayer which speaks of the precious gift of laughter:

Give me a sense of humour, Lord,
Give me the grace to see a joke,
To get some happiness from life
And pass it on to other folk.

THE FRIENDSHIP BOOK

A YOUNG American lawyer of the early 19th century was riding to court with his friends one day, when they saw on the ground two baby robins which had fallen from their nest. Mother robin was cheeping piteously as she fluttered overhead.

His friends rode on — but the young lawyer didn't. Eventually he rejoined them, and they chaffed him about his muddy boots and clothes.

He admitted that he'd put the two young robins back in their nest, and then added, "If I hadn't, I wouldn't have slept a wink all night."

Acts like this were second nature to the young man, Abraham Lincoln, later to become President of the United States of America.

WHAT wonderful work the Salvation Army does in the hostels for the homeless and the needy throughout the world. We'd all like to be a part of these compassionate, caring teams, wouldn't we?

However, it's not always possible — our everyday life has to go on, and all too often we have other commitments and responsibilities. That doesn't mean, though, that in our own small way we can't be a help, a comfort, to others in need.

Surely there have been times in your life when you have been helped and encouraged by just a kindly touch on the arm or shoulder, a warm smile, or a friendly greeting. All of these gave assurance that someone was thinking of us, someone cared. So take this as your motto today — pass it on — and then see someone else's face light up with hope and courage as you do so. It makes such a difference to know that someone cares.

THE FRIENDSHIP BOOK

THAT'S THE WAY!

WHAT a kindly wealth of comfort
We could show the world today,
If we spared a thought for others
As we meet them on our way!
If we made a special effort
Just to lend a helping hand,
Treating everyone as neighbours
Spreading friendship through the land.

Elizabeth Gozney.

AT a country house after dinner some wealthy guests were discussing their valuable collections. One man said, "I collect ancient gold coins. They are worth so much I keep them in a bank vault."

Another said, "I collect objects made of silver. I take them out now and then to have them cleaned, but they are stored in a secret safe in my home."

A third said, "I have a collection of rare china and I built a special strongroom to hold it."

At this point, one of the guests noticed that the servant clearing the table was smiling to himself. He pressed him to say why.

"Well, you see," said the servant, "I, too, am a collector. I collect the most precious things in the world and no one could ever steal them from me. I paid nothing for them and I carry them with me wherever I go, yet no one knows they are there or what they are."

"What are they?" his listeners demanded eagerly.

"My beautiful memories," he replied and, still smiling contentedly, left the room.

THE FRIENDSHIP BOOK

WHEN we go to London, the Lady of the House always looks for wild flowers — the ones that shoot up, almost in spite of themselves, between paving stones and on building sites, and other apparently barren areas. She seems to overlook all the beautiful window-boxes and leafy parks!

I recently drew her attention to a book I have been reading about London during the Second World War. One of the churches had been decorated for the Harvest Thanksgiving service, and near the altar was a huge sheaf of wheat. That evening the church was bombed and was reduced to a heap of rubble. Months later, out of the earth sprang green shoots, and soon a patch of wheat was growing.

I know now why the Lady of the House looks for beauty in dark places. It strengthens her belief that in the darkness and uncertainties of life we can always find some love, hope and affection — if only we look.

SUNDAY—APRIL 9.

AND let the peace of God rule in your hearts, to the which also ye are called in one body; and be ye thankful.

Colossians 3:15

MONDAY—APRIL 10.

LITTLE is remembered today of Edward E. Hale, the American preacher, except that he offered his followers this pattern for living:

To look up and not down,
To look forward and not back,
To look out and not in, and
To lend a hand.

It's still good advice, isn't it?

THE FRIENDSHIP BOOK

YOUNG Jamie likes to spend a day with us from time to time when his mother is busy. When asked what he would like to do after lunch, he nearly always says, "Can we go to the lake, please, Uncle Francis?" It's only a pond at the end of a woodland walk, but Jamie has spent many a happy hour pottering about there, collecting pebbles, tossing them into the water and watching the ripples spread.

It reminds me of the way acts of kindness spread, creating happiness amongst us.

Life may be taking us through a difficult patch, then along comes somebody new into our neighbourhood, our work place or our social circle, and tosses their own special "pebble" into the pool. What a difference it can make as its influence spreads and passes from one person to another in ever-widening circles.

It is good to be on the receiving end — and even better if we can be the one to toss a pebble of friendship to others!

DORIS CARTER shared with me another of her amusing stories about her grandfather's congregation. It concerns the old plumber and general help in the village.

He had not been in the habit of attending church regularly, so when he retired and started coming more often, Grandfather said, "I'm glad to see that now you're retired, you are coming to chapel every week."

However, the old man said cheerfully, "Oh, it's nothing to do with me retiring, Pastor. It's just that the Missis likes me out of the way while she cooks the Sunday dinner."

ABBEY BLOSSOM TIME

THE FRIENDSHIP BOOK

HOW easy it is to jog along in life in a safe way, never taking any chances, never taking any risks, and never venturing beyond our own narrow community, all sense of adventure and effort stifled. Cosy perhaps, safe — but how dull!

Yes, as a seafaring friend of mine once remarked: "A ship is safe in harbour, but that is not what it is built for!"

THIS Easter, I'm sure that many churches throughout the land will be decorated with beautiful white Madonna lilies.

Symbolising purity, the lily is dedicated to the Virgin Mary, but it is much older than that. Legend tells us that it first grew from the tears of Eve when she was cast out of the Garden of Eden. Certainly it had sacred associations long before Christ, and lilies were found painted on the walls of palaces in Crete 1500 years before his birth. At one time the "lilies of the field" which Jesus spoke about were thought to be anemones, but more recent research shows that they may have been Madonna lilies.

The early Christian Church adopted them as a symbol of purity, and when they were kept in a house it was believed that the occupants would be surrounded by an aura of holiness and protected from evil.

Nowadays, Madonna lilies, with all the lovely thoughts attached to them and described as "like saintly vestals, pale in prayer", are much sought after for weddings, flower festivals, and perhaps most of all, Easter.

THE FRIENDSHIP BOOK

IRIS HESSELDEN sent me these "Easter Blessings" which I have pinned to my desk:

May the promise of the Springtime, cheer you,
And the magic that it brings, thrill you;
May the healing of the sunlight, warm you,
And the blessings of Easter fill you.

May the peace of flowing waters, calm you,
And the strength of the hills, uphold you;
May the joy of waking earth, enrich you,
And the blessings of Easter enfold you.

May the music of the morning, lift you,
And the hope of all the world, guide you;
May the love of those you love, sustain you,
And the blessings of Easter stay beside you.

AND he said unto Jesus, Lord, remember me when thou comest into thy kingdom. And Jesus said unto him, Verily I say unto thee, Today shalt thou be with me in paradise.

Luke 23:42-43

AT an antique fair I picked up a small Staffordshire figure to examine it more closely. New, it probably cost less than a shilling, but the price I saw was £35. Age had added greatly to its value.

Now, I wonder how many of us can say that the years have added to our worth in the world?

THE FRIENDSHIP BOOK

WHEN I was younger I was a keen youth hosteller and got to know the various hostels well.

At one, there was a warden who seemed to be very bad-tempered. I now know that it was because she was so tired, but I must admit her demeanour used to be off-putting. However, she'd cooked some superb meals during our stay, and we all enjoyed tucking into her wholesome and plentiful fare.

One morning, I was about to leave the dining-room, but something made me turn back, to thank her. She saw me and a look on her face said, "What does he want now?" I praised her cooking and all that she had done to make us comfortable. For a fleeting moment a smile lit up her face, and all her tiredness vanished.

A word of thanks and appreciation costs nothing — but it can mean a great deal.

A WISE man was known to be writing a book, but the years went by and he was still a long way from reaching the last page. One day, when he was very old, a young man asked him if he was not impatient to see it completed.

The old man smiled. "All my life it has been my ambition to finish writing my book, but an ambition realised is like a snowflake in a warm hand. Take away my dream and what would I have left?"

When he died, his pen was still in his hand, the unfinished manuscript in front of him. It is said he was smiling happily.

If the story has a moral, it is this: don't take away people's hopes and dreams. Often they are the most precious and best-loved things in their lives.

WHO NEEDS A BRIDGE?

D

THE FRIENDSHIP BOOK

KEN DODD has been a popular and successful comedian for many years. He has worked hard at perfecting his act to create an eccentric appearance, while making sure that his jokes are suitable for family entertainment. To watch people rolling in their seats with laughter is quite infectious!

However, he has a serious side to his character, too. Discussing what makes us happy, he believes that the secret lies in being creative. For him it is using the gift of laughter and being able to see the funny side of things, and he has developed this talent to make people feel better.

Being creative comes in many shapes and sizes. For some of us it could be in making a garden, organising a playgroup, singing in a choir, joining a drama group, or it could be in creating a home and bringing up a happy family. The key is not how big our opportunities are, but how we use the ones we have been given.

SOME time ago, an eminent speaker was talking about the mess that the world sometimes appears to be in, and went on to relate a story from Africa.

A man called John Simmonds took his wife and mother-in-law on safari. One night there was a great commotion outside the tents. Investigating, John saw a large lion facing his mother-in-law, who, not surprisingly, was screaming.

Mrs Simmonds cried out, "John, John, what are you going to do?"

"Do?" he replied. "Why, nothing. After all, the lion got himself into this mess so he must get himself out of it!"

E

THE FRIENDSHIP BOOK

YOU think little things don't matter? Then consider these: a sneeze can start an avalanche; a pinprick will set a horse galloping; diseases are spread by germs invisible to the human eye.

On the beneficial side, a pen and a scrap of paper are all that's needed for signing a peace treaty to end war; a slim gold band seals a marriage; a light kiss says "I love you!"

Yes, as the song says, "Little things mean a lot."

BUT he said, Yea rather, blessed are they that hear the word of God, and keep it.

Luke 11:28

I HAVE spent many happy hours solving — or trying to solve — crossword puzzles. At times it is entirely a case of *trying* to solve, especially with difficult cryptic puzzles.

I admire those clever people who seem to be able to work out difficult clues in no time at all. I am full of admiration, too, for a Fijian lady I read about who got her name in *The Guinness Book Of Records.* She wrote to *The Times* to announce that she had completed one of their crosswords after working at it for 34 years. A record of great perseverance indeed, and I can imagine her feeling of triumph as she filled in the last clue!

It illustrates once again the old saying about difficult tasks taking a long time and the impossible a little longer. If you like, it's the story of Bruce and the spider with a modern touch.

THE FRIENDSHIP BOOK

WHEN I called to see our old friend Mary, she was sitting on a bench in her small back garden with "The Fireside Book" anthology of poetry on her knee.

"It was a birthday present, Francis," she said, "and I think it has become the favourite of all my books. There is something here to match every one of my moods — poems that are beautiful, sad, amusing, joyful or thought-provoking.

"At bed-time I pick out a few of the ones I have come to love particularly and I know that reading them will leave lovely thoughts in my mind and help me to drift off into peaceful sleep."

As I have often said before, a visit to Mary always leaves me with something to think about. When I got home I looked up something that I remembered Coleridge had written on the subject: "Poetry has been to me its own exceeding great reward. It has given me the habit of wishing to discover the good and the beautiful in all that meets and surrounds me."

A lovely sentiment indeed!

GIVING

"WHAT, giving again?"
    I asked in a daze,
"And must I keep giving,
    And giving always?"
"Oh, no," said the angel
    Whose eyes pierced me through:
"Just stop when the Saviour
    Stops giving to you!"
              Anon.

SPRING DELIGHT

THE FRIENDSHIP BOOK

THE Lord's my Shepherd, I'll not want;
He makes me down to lie
In pastures green; he leadeth me
The quiet waters by.

So begins one of our most familiar and best-loved hymns. Yet it might never have become so well known had it not been for a young schoolgirl, Jessie Irving, who lived in the fishing town of Fraserburgh early last century.

One day she came home from school with the task, as homework, of composing music to set to one of the psalms. The one she chose was Psalm 23, and the music she wrote for it she named Crimond — after the nearby village.

Ninety years later Princess Elizabeth, as she was then, popularised it when she chose it for one of her wedding hymns in Westminster Abbey and since then many brides and grooms have wanted it at their own wedding.

With its beautiful melody, the words of comfort, peace and assurance, and the constant promise of sunshine breaking through, it is not surprising that it has become many people's favourite hymn.

NEXT time you are asked for advice and find yourself stumped for a truly helpful reply, try to remember this verse I came across in an American magazine. I don't know who wrote it, but it's a little masterpiece:

His thoughts were slow,
His words were few, and never formed to glisten.
But he was such a joy to all his friends —
You should have heard him listen.

THE FRIENDSHIP BOOK

"THE Friendship Book" is read all over the world, and I was delighted to receive a letter from Florence O. Force in Park Ridge, Illinois. She told me: "I was going over old papers and came across some notes I wrote in 1927, taken from our Church Girls' Paper, and telling about a women's group in Cuba. They had set themselves guidelines which they headed Ten Commandments of the Modern Woman:

1. To be as true and clear as a drop of dew.
2. To be as strong as a thread of silk, which may be stretched, but will not break.
3. To be as upright as a palm tree in the fields.
4. To be as simple as the lark, which has only one song.
5. To have an ideal which will be a shield.
6. To be as active and hard working as the bee.
7. To be as generous as a ray of sunshine.
8. To accept life with serenity and joy.
9. To rise above the bitterness of unhappy hours.
10. Not to fear sorrow.

"As a teenager these influenced me greatly, and they surely have as much meaning nowadays," Mrs Force reflects.

I agree wholeheartedly!

AND keep the charge of the Lord thy God, to walk in his ways, to keep his statutes, and his commandments, and his judgments, and his testimonies, as it is written in the law of Moses, that thou mayest prosper in all that thou doest, and whithersoever thou turnest thyself.

Kings I 2:3

MAY

SEND ME A SIGN

SEND me a sign, Lord,
Show me the way
To a happy tomorrow,
A brighter new day.

Send me a sign, Lord,
Lead where you will,
No matter the terrain,
I'll follow you still.

Send me a sign, Lord,
Show me you care.
I can face any foe, Lord,
Just knowing you're there!

Glenda Moore.

A LITTLE while ago, two young neighbours, Mark and Daniel, were avid viewers of a series of Laurel and Hardy films, which were being shown on television every Saturday morning.

One weekend, a bridal car appeared outside the house opposite. I noticed the children's mother at the window watching for the bride — but though she waited and waited, the girl took a long time to appear.

Then young Mark came out with what seemed to him a perfectly acceptable reason for the bride's delay: "Perhaps she doesn't want to miss Laurel and Hardy, either!"

WOODLAND WONDER

THE FRIENDSHIP BOOK

WEDNESDAY—MAY 3.

THE National Garden Festival at Ebbw Vale in 1992 was the fifth and final one. Previous locations were at Liverpool, Stoke-on-Trent, Glasgow and Gateshead, and all were situated in areas of industrial blight in order to create places of beauty from derelict sites.

In the 1970s and 1980s, 12,000 jobs had been lost in Ebbw Vale when the steelworks and coal mines closed, and this unpromising area was designated for the Festival. It took five years of planning and construction, creating thousands of jobs.

Almost two million cubic yards of sludge had to be shifted before the once-blackened floor of the valley was made green with an array of trees, shrubs, plants and bulbs.

When opening day arrived, the area was ablaze with daffodils which had been specially retarded in a cold store.

At the end of the Festival, it was decided that the site must not be allowed to relapse into its former state. The lake and much of the landscaping were retained, and a village was planned with new houses and flats for sale or rental. A thousand permanent jobs were created in small industrial units.

It's proof that practicality and beauty *can* go hand in hand, bringing all the benefits that both can offer.

THURSDAY—MAY 4.

THESE beautiful words are translated from an old book of Gaelic wisdom and lore:

"With love, no harm can come. Do not forget, ever, the light that is shining ahead of you, calling on you to look ever upwards. Be guided and guarded in all your ways by the spirit of love."

FRIDAY—MAY 5.

WHEN he died, Seton Gordon, the superb naturalist, left a diary in which he had scribbled these words:

"The inner side of every cloud is bright and shining — therefore turn my cloud about so I may always wear it inside-out."

SATURDAY—MAY 6.

THE foreground of life depends on the background. When you sit down to watch television and relax, do you ever think of all the hard work and thought that has been put into the programme? The script, the actors, the lighting and the actual recording, all have to make a perfect mix.

A fulfilled life, too, should be well thought out. Most things are achieved successfully if they are well prepared. A marathon runner prepares long before the race, and for even a short performance a dedicated musician practises for weeks beforehand.

Robert Baden-Powell, founder of the Scout Movement, always spoke and wrote about being prepared — "Be Prepared" was his motto. He knew that being prepared for the small things in life would lead youngsters to practise the habit consistently to meet great challenges with courage, the tasks of life with strength, and even its disasters with a measure of serenity.

SUNDAY—MAY 7.

THIS is a faithful saying, and worthy of all acceptation, that Christ Jesus came into the world to save sinners; of whom I am chief.

Timothy I 1:15

THE FRIENDSHIP BOOK

THE TROUBLE WITH ME

THE trouble with her — she thinks she's in charge,
Her lips are too bright, her hips are too large.
The trouble with him — he's mousy and small,
But thinks that he's well dressed, handsome and tall.
The trouble with them — it's easy to see,
They notice my faults and the trouble with me!

Iris Hesselden.

WE all treasure memories of happy times in our lives. Sometimes we are reminded of these by the simplest of things — an old song, a fading photograph, a face glimpsed in a crowd, a child's well-loved toy.

Writing earlier this century the author H. Mortimer Batten told of the beautiful way by which a Red Indian would bring fond recollections to mind:

"When he is superlatively happy, when he is living through a moment which he wishes to be able to recall for all time, he takes a sweet-smelling root, or a herb, crushes it in his hands, and inhales its scent, till it is indelibly stamped upon his memory as part of that phase of his life. Thus, in the wallet of an Indian you will find all manner of oddments, a dried flower or a root with a strange aroma, and in moments of sadness or idleness, he is able, with their aid, to recall the happiest incidents of his life."

It is another example of the wisdom of a fine race that many were once foolish enough to regard as savages!

COUNTRY CALM

THE FRIENDSHIP BOOK

"I SEE you haven't managed to complete the crossword today, Francis," said my friend George. He had called in for a chat one night and had glanced at the newspaper lying beside him on the settee.

"No," I replied, "it's a difficult one so I've left it for the time being. I'll go and put on the kettle and you can have a look at it to see what *you* can make of it."

When I returned with the cups, George informed me that he had solved two more clues, so we put our heads together and by the time we had drunk our tea, we had finished the puzzle as well.

As with so many other things, two heads are better than one, and a trouble shared is a trouble halved. In most of life's problems a friend who has time to sit with us and talk things through can usually help to put things in the right perspective. It's good when we have a friend like that — and good when we can be one in turn. As an Ethiopian proverb says: "When spiders' webs unite they can tie up a lion."

FROM time to time a friend sends me her church service sheet which often contains a verse or thought for the day. Here is one that I feel sure will interest you:

God give you more than you can ever think or ask;
God use you far beyond the soundings of your task;
God lead you farther than the vision yet can see;
God mould you day by day more perfectly.
God bless you — in the way he seeth best,
God bless you, that each life YOU touch be blest.

It's an encouraging message of hope for us all, whatever our problems.

THE FRIENDSHIP BOOK

*T*AKE *one step at a time, a day at a time,*
  And leave to God the rest,
Think not of years, that are still to come,
But do this day your best—
With head held high, and a purpose true,
Fulfil every task awaiting you.

A day at a time, an hour at a time,
Fill now with kindly deeds,
This is enough for your heart to know,
Help in another's needs—
The road is long, so don't try to see
How steep the path that is yet to be.

Give a smile at a time, a song at a time,
To those who may this day
Need a light to cheer some dreary spot,
A lantern's friendly ray.
Only in days are we given strength,
To reach the top of the hill at length.

Margaret H. Dixon.

SOMETIMES I have to chuckle at the unintended humour of folk not born in the United Kingdom, in their struggles to master our language.

Jennie has recently left school, and managed to obtain a job with a firm whose managing director was from Hungary, and came to this country some years ago.

As he welcomed Jennie into his organisation, he gave her a warm greeting: "We're very happy to have you with us. As you know, we're a little underhanded."

THE FRIENDSHIP BOOK

AND I will set my tabernacle among you; and my soul shall not abhor you. And I will walk among you, and will be your God, and ye shall be my people.

Leviticus 26:11-12

FEW weeks go by without us being reminded of the grinding poverty in many parts of the world. Newspaper adverts constantly appeal for our help and television reports bring home to us the awful suffering of disease and starvation in countries where there is drought. It's a salutary reminder that millions of the poorest people in the world are still without the basic necessities of life.

Shortly, thousands of volunteers will be setting out on door-to-door collections and many others will be skipping their own lunch, or baking for cake stalls, in order to raise money to save lives.

It will mark the start of Christian Aid Week, when particular attention is focused on those who so desperately need our help. It's an appeal that we just can't ignore.

HAVE you ever thought of the important role doors fill in our lives?

We can close them behind us and turn the key in the lock, cutting ourselves off from the world.

Or we can open them wide to friends and neighbours, and use them ourselves to go out and about in the community.

Is yours a keep-out door or a come-and-go door? I certainly hope there is always a welcome on *our* mat!

F

THE FRIENDSHIP BOOK

WE are all responsible for the influence of our example. How is *your* example recognised?

In the home by kindness?
In business by honesty?
In society by courtesy?
In work by thoroughness?
In play by fairness?

FROM the pen of a poet come these thoughtful words:

It was only a cup of water with a gentle grace bestowed,
But it cheered the lonely traveller upon life's dusty road.
None noticed the cup of water as a beautiful act of love,
Save the angels keeping the records, away in the land above.
The trifles in secret given, the prayer in the quiet night,
And the little unnoticed nothings are great in our Saviour's sight!

CHANGE comes to us all at various stages of life. Sometimes we welcome it, but all too often we fear it — it is the fear of the unknown, isn't it? Well, don't fear change, no matter how suddenly it might materialise.

Remember — no river ever flowed that didn't, at times, burst its banks and take a new course. Life is a river, so go with it, not against it.

THE FRIENDSHIP BOOK

I DON'T know who wrote this poem entitled "It Doesn't Always Follow". It is one I copied down some time ago and although it may not be the greatest of poetry, I feel there is quite a lot of truth in it.

> *It isn't the man who knows the most*
> *Who has the most to say;*
> *Nor yet the one who's wealthiest*
> *Who gives the most away.*

> *It isn't the bird in the gilded cage*
> *Who sings the sweetest song,*
> *Nor yet the girl who's prettiest*
> *That's faithful, true and strong.*

H E that cometh from above is above all: he that is of the earth is earthly, and speaketh of the earth: he that cometh from heaven is above all.

John 3:31

JAMES, aged 84, left his small village in the Highlands to spend a few days in Blackpool.

As he queued for a tram he watched in suspense as the pole came off the wire and the tram stopped.

A moment later James turned to the person behind him, who happened to be a clergyman, and said with a smile, "You know, Reverend, it just shows that if we lose contact with the Power Above, life comes to an immediate standstill."

I'm sure the parson recognised the seeds of a sermon contained in the old man's remark.

THE FRIENDSHIP BOOK

TAKE MY PEN, LORD

*T*AKE my pen, Lord,
  Help me write the words within my heart,
Guide my hand across the empty page,
Take my thoughts and harness them with love.
Let the lines be comforting and warm,
And so reach out and touch a seed of hope.
Take my pen, Lord,
Let the words illuminate the dark,
And like a little candle, light the night.

Iris Hesselden.

NEXT time you start to grumble about having to go out in the rain, just remember how a heavy shower inspired one of the most joyous popular songs ever written, "Singing In The Rain".

Then go out, doing exactly that — even it it's just to yourself.

"SIMON, what would you like for your tenth birthday?" a friend asked his grandson recently.

The boy thought hard for a moment and then said "a tree, please!"

Surprised, his grandfather asked why.

"So that when I'm old there'll be trees for children to look at and climb," the boy smiled.

Simon got his tree, and I'm pleased to tell you it's growing well.

I don't think we have to worry too much about the future of this planet as long as there are children like Simon.

FRIDAY—MAY 26

DO you like books? Of course you do, or you wouldn't be reading this one!

John Wilson, a 19th-century bookseller, wrote:

A jolly good book wherein to look
Is better to me than gold.

James Thomson, the poet, said:

Give a man a pipe he can smoke,
Give a man a book he can read,
And his home is bright with a calm delight
Though the room be poor indeed.

Nearer home, our friend Mary once said to me, "Give me a good book, Francis, and you can throw everything else out of the window."

A bit drastic, perhaps, but I know how she feels!

SATURDAY—MAY 27.

I LIKE the story told of the famous Italian tenor Enrico Caruso.

His biographer records that he was "never a victim of the mean temper which degrades opponents in order to enjoy a cheap triumph. He was generous in advice and assistance to fellow artistes. When he was singing with an artiste of less vocal power, he would modulate his sonorous voice that he might not overwhelm the less fortunate singer."

Consideration for others is the very essence of friendship, isn't it?

SUNDAY—MAY 28.

O LORD our Lord, how excellent is thy name in all the earth! who hast set thy glory above the heavens.

Psalms 8:1

THE FRIENDSHIP BOOK

D INAH MULOCK CRAIG wrote a book which became a classic. "John Halifax, Gentleman" was the story of a poor orphan boy who made good by his own integrity and honest dealings.

Recently, I came across one of her pearls of wisdom:

"The secret of life is not to do what one likes, but to try to like that which one has to do; and one does like it — in time."

It's all to do with the value of dogged persistence — and determination.

A MOTHER'S THOUGHTS

T WO chubby arms outstretched to me
A little, winsome smile,
Who could resist this wordless plea
To pick him up a while?

My baby to a man must grow
To travel far and wide,
May winds of fortune gently blow
And God be by his side.

Dorothy M. Loughran.

I HAD a letter from Waltraud Klose, a reader in Germany. Among other matters was a short, but nevertheless profound saying which I think you'll appreciate. It is simply this: "Never start stopping."

Something positive to bear in mind when life becomes a little too hectic!

JUNE

THURSDAY—JUNE 1.

WHEN my eye catches a weed or two flourishing in the garden, I console myself by recalling the naturalist W. H. Hudson, who was brought up in the wide open spaces of the Argentine. He grew to love the English countryside when he came to Britain, but was appalled by the over-neat gardens.

He told how, staying as a guest at a large country house, he fled the manicured lawns and precise flower beds in search of a wild corner where a profusion of plants grew as they wanted to.

One man's weeds are another man's wild flowers, aren't they?

I have to report, though, that this excuse cuts little ice, or should I say grass, with the Lady of the House!

FRIDAY—JUNE 2.

AS a change from the usual competitions aimed at children, one of our local church magazines ran one for the over-sixties. The idea came from a magazine article called "Fun In Little Things".

Senior citizens were invited to submit a short list of activities that gave them pleasure. What a variety there was — barbecues, berry-picking expeditions, photography, birdwatching, making greetings cards and notelets from recycled material, painting, writing poetry, playing Scrabble and counting blessings, all indicating that there are a lot of lively minds amongst the older generation.

The lesson here is that if we can no longer do the things we used to enjoy, let's try enjoying the things we can still do.

THE FRIENDSHIP BOOK

SATURDAY—JUNE 3.

TOMORROW is another Sabbath. What will you do with it? It was given to us as a day of rest, and how grateful ordinary folk used to be for the one day in the week when there was respite from grinding work!

George Herbert, living at the beginning of the 17th century, called it "O day, most calm, most bright". Over 100 years later, the poet James Grahame wrote, "Hail, Sabbath! thee I hail, the poor man's day."

Well, "Sunday, sweet Sunday" is with us still, and thank God for that. We can use it as we will; we can waste it, fritter it away, or we can do what He intended: restore our minds and our bodies so that they are ready to face another week.

SUNDAY—JUNE 4.

FROM that time Jesus began to preach, and to say, Repent: for the kingdom of heaven is at hand.

Matthew 4:17

MONDAY—JUNE 5.

TODAY, I'd like to share these points to ponder with you:

When you think that life's not fair, then remember God is there!

If God sends us on stony paths, he provides us with strong boots.

I am not afraid of tomorrow, for I have seen yesterday and I love today.

THE FRIENDSHIP BOOK

I WAS having a particularly busy time, but it was a glorious day so I decided to set out for the park.

For about an hour I watched children feeding the ducks, then I sauntered across to the rose garden for a leisurely picnic. Finally, I moved to a little pool where the splashing of the fountain in the cool water completed my relaxation. I didn't achieve any more work that day, but, oh, how this spell outdoors recharged my batteries!

Time taken away from the routine and worry of everyday life is precious. The novelist R. Murray Gilchrist wrote: "A lordly pleasure for a lazy man is to rest beside the pools and to watch the stealthy glidings of the great trout between the waving weeds", while Romany of the BBC had this to say: "When you get fed up with present-day happenings, go out into the lanes and the fields, and listen and look at the things of Nature. There is no hurry in that world — that is why I am a dodderer . . . To be a dodderer is a lost art these days, one that we should recapture."

I heartily agree.

WEDNESDAY—JUNE 7.

A YOUNG minister had a visitor whom he had tried to help when she was going through a bad patch some time before.

She had been impressed in particular by one of the messages he had passed on, and now she told the minister how much it had encouraged her. It was a line from a "Spiritual Guide" issued in 1675 by the Spanish priest Miguel de Molinos.

I think you'll agree that it's worth quoting again:

"For he who rises quickly and continues his race is as if he had never fallen."

THE FRIENDSHIP BOOK

I SET MY SAILS

I SET my sails to the wind and breeze,
To the crested waves of Summer seas,
I set my sails, and I steer my way,
To where there is neither night nor day.

I set my sails all pure and white,
Which billow out to my delight,
While the sea birds cry and follow me,
Spreading their wings for the open sea.

I set my sails, and there on high,
The clouds sail, too, in a pale blue sky,
They travel fast and are more free
Than I below on this tossing sea.

I set my sails to Eternity,
With the winds of God directing me,
I set my sails to a purpose true,
To seek for Heaven in the distant blue.

Margaret H. Dixon.

YOUNG Robert was reluctant to stop playing in the garden when his mother called him for a bath and bed. However, when I suggested that I should do the honours on this occasion, he appeared with alacrity.

Once Robert was washed, dried and in his pyjamas, I pointed to the bath and said, "You certainly needed a bath tonight, Robert. Just look at that tidemark!"

Giving me an aggrieved look he said, "That wasn't all me, Uncle Francis! I sat in the middle."

THERE is one phrase in particular which I feel is much overused these days: "Of course (s)he is over the hill at that age."

This suggests that by a certain time you are more or less too old to achieve anything worthwhile.

Of course this is simply not true — you would never have found Wordsworth, Rembrandt or Beethoven subscribing to the idea, for they were creating great works late into life.

In our own lifetime, there was a lady of 58 who dearly wanted to obtain a university degree, but felt too old to try. To a professor who encouraged her to commence studies, she complained, "But I'll be 62 when I get my degree!"

"How old will you be if you *don't* get it?" was the reply. Then she began to see that her mentor's argument made sense, and she decided to enrol in the course of her choice as soon as possible.

We still reach our allotted age, whatever that is going to be, so why not enrich our lives on the way?

SUNDAY—JUNE 11.

O Lord, thou art my God; I will exalt thee, I will praise thy name; for thou hast done wonderful things, thy counsels of old are faithfulness and truth.

Isaiah 25:1

MONDAY—JUNE 12.

HAS it ever struck you that we spend half our lives in daylight and half in darkness? In the same way there is a balance in all our lives of happy hours and sad ones. Just remember that nights are needed as well as days to mellow the orchards.

THE FRIENDSHIP BOOK

COLOURS

*F*ROWNS *can make the start of day*
A really dreary kind of grey.
But a smile is sunshine's gold
So will you today a smile unfold?
A smile — and this will make you think —
Puts you — and others — in the pink!

Elizabeth Gozney.

HAVE you ever seen the beautiful "Morning Glory"? Its brilliant sky-blue flowers open early in the morning, but by afternoon they have closed again. I like the interesting little legend that's attached to it.

There was once a princess who used to enjoy sitting in her garden amongst the flowers. Because she was so delicate, she had to return to the palace before the day became hot, and so she never saw those certain varieties of flowers which didn't open until the sun shone on them.

This made her very sad, and one day, as she returned to the palace, she shed a few tears — and each one that fell to the ground turned into a little seed. A few weeks later, as the princess walked in her garden in the early morning she was surprised to find a beautiful new flower growing all around her — climbing up the garden wall, twining round the trees and cascading over arches.

She was overjoyed, and since that day the name Morning Glory has been given to the flower that sprang from the tears of a princess's blue eyes.

THE FRIENDSHIP BOOK

MARK TWAIN, the American writer, tells the story of his small daughter who had been breaking her heart over what had seemed to her young mind utter disasters — a cancelled picnic and a broken toy. Several times her mother said to her, "Susy, you mustn't cry over little things."

The little girl thought about her mother's words, but they baffled her. At last she went to her mother for help. "Mamma, what is 'little things'?" she asked.

How often we, as adults, think that a child is making a fuss about nothing. We forget that what may appear trivial to us, can be of great importance to a child. It isn't true only of children, either, is it? All too often we think someone else is "making a lot of fuss about nothing." Well, it may appear to be nothing to us, but to the person involved it is everything at that moment.

No wonder being tolerant of others is such a tough test of personality! It is surely one of the virtues that is most admirable in others.

NOBODY can avoid suffering at some time, and often we are tempted to ask why misfortune should happen to us. However, through this experience so much of the warmth, understanding and compassion inherent in us all can emerge, if we'll just let it work that way.

Sir Edward Elgar, the great composer, was aware of this. One day he sat listening to a young singer who sang with faultless technique and marvellous tone. "She *is* good," he said afterwards, "but not great. When something happens in her life to touch her heart, she will be great."

THE FRIENDSHIP BOOK

WHAT'S the shortest speech you've ever heard? When tea first reached Braemar, a shopkeeper invited customers to come and taste it.

They crowded into his premises where he stood behind the counter arrayed with cups and saucers. He boiled a big kettle, poured the water over the tea leaves and then, after a decent interval, raised the result above his head. "Ladies and gentlemen," he announced, "Teapot!"

If only all speeches were as brief and to the point!

SUNDAY—JUNE 18.

FOR God hath not given us the spirit of fear; but of power, and of love, and of a sound mind.

Timothy II 1:7

MONDAY—JUNE 19.

OUR language is not one of the easiest to learn and I can sympathise with our foreign friends who make mistakes. In this context, I recall reading a story about a reception given by Lord Lonsdale.

An Eastern diplomat, taking his leave, said to his host, "I must not cockroach on your time any longer."

As he ushered him to the door, Lord Lonsdale congratulated the diplomat on his command of English, then added quietly, "I should point out a tiny slip — the word should be 'encroach'."

The guest promptly made a diplomatic reply, "Forgive me, I was addressing you personally and therefore used 'cockroach'. If I had been addressing her ladyship I would certainly have used the feminine, 'henroach'."

Diplomats are never lost for an explanation!

F

THE FRIENDSHIP BOOK

I OFTEN think of old Benjamin, who used to sit in the back pew of his little country chapel.

My friend Eric used to visit the chapel to lead worship, and there was no mistaking the welcome that old Benjamin used to give: "I've bin reckoning on yer coming."

Eric always used to say that old Benjamin's welcome always got him off to a good start.

On another occasion recently I overheard old Benjamin talking to the minister after the service. He thanked him for his sermon, and for speaking up so that even the slightly deaf could hear. Then he remarked how much good the minister's visit had done for Mrs Benjamin, who was almost housebound.

We can't do without the Benjamins of this world. If a word of encouragement was needed, he wouldn't hesitate to give it. Now, don't we all react positively to a bit of appreciation?

MORNING

THE lazy man said,
Turning over in bed,
"Today's going to be such a bore,
The time will pass slow
For I've no place to go
And nothing to do any more."

The busy man said,
As he leaped out of bed,
"Today there's so much to be done,
The time will flash by,
The minutes just fly,
For I'm going to be having such fun!"

THE FRIENDSHIP BOOK

WE have several large terracotta pots in our garden, some holding bulbs, others herbs.

One day I noticed that one of the pots had cracked and large pieces had broken off, though fortunately the remainder was still whole. The broken pot held my parsley plants and I was very surprised to find that the soil in the pot was still in position, although there was nothing at all to hold it in place. As the soil was intact and that was the life giver, the parsley continued to flourish.

We are rather like the terracotta pots, aren't we? Even when our bodies are not as fit as we'd like, completely well, we are still capable of making much of our lives, and giving out love and encouragement to others. If we dispense the healing touch, we will do much to make *ourselves* whole.

WHENEVER we see the initials VC, we usually think of those gallant folk who were awarded the Victoria Cross for bravery in war.

However, I was informed recently that VC can also stand for Very Cheerful.

The best time to show a cheerful spirit is when things become difficult. I remember a gentleman who, in spite of diabetes and other problems, maintained a very happy frame of mind. When he died, one of our mutual friends admitted that when he was in Harry's company, "I felt in the presence of a saint — and somehow he made *you* feel a saint, too, or at least that you *ought* to try to be one."

Somehow, the spirit of the Very Cheerful rubs off on others, so that they become the better for the happy contact.

THE FRIENDSHIP BOOK

TODAY is Midsummer's Day, and the Feast of St John the Baptist. In her book "British Folk Customs", Christina Hole writes about an old custom of the season, the Peace and Good Neighbourhood Dinner held at Kidderminster.

The idea began around 500 years ago when a lady left money to her neighbours in Church Street to provide a loaf of bread at Midsummer for each child living there. She also expressed a wish that all the men in the street should meet in friendship on the same day to settle any disputes in the past year.

In the 1700s another resident of Church Street left money to supplement the bequest and extend gifts to men and women alike who attended on Midsummer Evening, in order to foster "the better establishment and continuance of the said Friendly Meeting for Ever."

These bequests became the foundation of the Peace and Good Neighbourhood Dinner, held each year at Midsummer. The chairman tries to reconcile anyone who is at odds with his neighbour, and the toast of the evening is "Peace and Good Neighbourhood."

Long may it prosper!

THIS is my commandment, That ye love one another, as I have loved you.

John 15:12

HOW can you tell good from bad? A wise man once remarked that he had never known a good thing that was not beautiful, or a bad thing that was not ugly. It makes identification easier, doesn't it?

BUTTERCUP MEADOW

THE FRIENDSHIP BOOK

OUR friend Ann often comes to see us, but on one occasion we hadn't seen her for a while and were eager to catch up on all her news.

This particular day she was bubbling over with something special to tell us, having recently been to a reunion at her old school, 60 miles away. It had been many years since she'd seen the girls she had been at school with, and Ann told us that she had wondered whether she would recognise them — and whether *they* would recognise *her*!

It had been a great success, and, yes, they had all managed to recognise each other. Hair was grey in most cases, but the faces were the same and so were the voices. Few had fulfilled all their schoolgirl dreams, but most were happy to reminisce about school life and to exchange chat about their husbands, children and grandchildren. All were determined to meet up again quite soon.

When Ann had gone home, I thought that even if youthful ambitions had not all been realised, it was good to feel that the joys of family life are the lasting important values.

WHILE reading about antiquities it brought to mind a verse I know:
We see by the light of thousands of years,
And the knowledge of millions of men;
The lessons they learned through blood and in tears,
Are ours for the reading and then
We swear at their errors, and follies, and dreams,
Their frail idols of wood and of stone,
And call ourselves wiser, forgetting, it seems,
That the future may laugh at our own.

THE FRIENDSHIP BOOK

ALBERT worked for the council, but his hobby was sketching, especially churches. He took every available opportunity in his spare time to go and draw, capturing the architectural details with great care. He used to take his grandson Donald along with him, and he encouraged the boy to study his surroundings in as much detail as possible.

"Look up! Look up!" he would urge. "You will see very little of interest down *there*."

Donald continued to do precisely that, and in his autobiography recollects that although he occasionally treads on something nasty on the pavement, that has been a very small price to pay for the pleasures he has had from "looking up".

He remarks that the top of a tree fretted against the sky is so much more beautiful than the pavement at your feet, so much so that every childhood walk down the High Street seemed to be packed with adventure and discovery.

Donald has continued to look up all his life, and he is also esteemed as one of Britain's best-known actors — Donald Sinden.

I CAN'T resist browsing among racks of second-hand books in charity shops and bookshops. I had an unexpected reward the other morning when I picked up the classic novel "The Cloister And The Hearth" by Charles Reade, and in the first chapter I read:

"Not a day passes but men and women of no note do great deeds, speak great words, and suffer noble sorrow."

What a grand thought with which to begin a day!

JULY

SATURDAY—JULY 1.

I LIKE this story about young Mark, though I am sure there are many other little boys just like him.

Whenever it was time to go to bed, he always protested loudly, so one day his mother thought she would teach him a lesson.

Taking him to the henhouse at the bottom of the garden, she pointed to the chicks who immediately ran under the wing of the roosting hen as soon as she clucked.

Mark agreed that the chicks were obedient, then added, "But their mother goes to bed first!"

SUNDAY—JULY 2.

A ND he saith unto them, Follow me, and I will make you fishers of men.

Matthew 4:19

MONDAY—JULY 3.

I T'S a familiar saying that money is the root of all evil. It doesn't need to be. Used properly it can do nothing but good. In his great novel about South Africa, "Cry, The Beloved Country", Alan Paton writes:

"Money is not something to go mad about, and throw your hat in the air for. Money is for food and clothes and comfort, and a visit to the pictures. Money is to make happy the lives of children. Money is for security, and for dreams, and for hopes, and for purposes. Money is for buying the fruits of the earth, of the land where you were born."

If it was used only for such good things as these, what a happier and more contented place the world would be!

BLUE HEAVEN

THE FRIENDSHIP BOOK

SOME time ago, Josephine Walker of Bradford reached her 21st birthday, and wondered how best to celebrate. She didn't want to be selfish and have the day all to herself. Then she had a remarkable idea . . .

At the end of her birthday, Josephine spoke of what had been the happiest day of her whole life so far. She had hired a coach and taken a party of underprivileged children for a day's outing to York. The weather was sunny, they all had a wonderful time, and when it was over, Josephine remarked that she would remember sharing her day, and remember those 30 radiant faces, as long as she lived.

By helping others to enjoy life, we will gain a great deal of added pleasure, too.

MOST of us enjoy going on holiday, and at this time of the year many will be looking forward to packing our suitcases. However, once our break is over, there is nothing so satisfying as seeing our own front door again. After all, home is where the heart is.

Dr Samuel Johnson considered that "to be happy at home is the ultimate result of all ambitions", while novelist George Eliot wrote: "Few are born to do great work in the world, but the work that all men can do is to make a small home circle brighter and better."

Perhaps the sentiment nearest to my own feelings is expressed in the words given to Charles Pooter in Grossmith's "Diary Of A Nobody". "After my work in the city," he remarks, "I like to be at home. What's the good of a home if you are never in it? Home, Sweet Home, that's my motto."

Hear, hear!

H

THE FRIENDSHIP BOOK

I LIKE the story of a security-conscious Vatican official.

When he heard that Pope John Paul II was proposing to take a daily walk in his garden, he hastened to reassure the Holy Father that arrangements had been made to screen his path from the view of nearby residents.

"Why?" asked the Pope with a twinkle in his eye. "Don't I look respectable?"

EARLY last Summer, the Lady of the House bought a packet of night-scented stock seeds and planted them in large containers in the back garden. With interest I watched them grow — spindly green shoots topped with faded little flowers.

"They don't seem to be doing very well," I remarked. "Will we replace them with something colourful — geraniums or fuchsias perhaps?"

"Oh, no, Francis," said the Lady of the House. "Come outside at dusk and you'll be surprised."

Sure enough, the flowers that had looked so drab in the daytime against the brighter flowers had really come into their own. The petals which had previously looked so shrivelled, were fully open and a pinkish mauve, while the scent was lovely.

It made me think of the passing of the years. We may be noticing our waning energy; that we are getting hard of hearing; even that we are losing our powers of concentration. However, in compensation many things increase. We will likely have grown in kindness, patience, tolerance, serenity and the ability to forgive. They are lovely characteristics — and are usually at their best in the evening of our lives!

THE FRIENDSHIP BOOK

SHIP-SHAPE

WHAT ship can steer us through Life's sea
  Of turbulence and stress?
What ship can always guarantee
  A quest for happiness?
What ship can ascertain the kind
  Of course to be explored?
The ship to sail into the mind
  Is FRIENDSHIP — All Aboard!

J. M. Robertson.

THE Lord is my rock, and my fortress, and my deliverer, my God, my strength, in whom I will trust; my buckler, and the horn of my salvation, and my high tower.

Psalms 18:2

OF all forms of humour, I think the simple unconscious remark of the laughter-provoking kind is one of the best. I don't know if this story, taken from the local newspaper, is true, but I certainly found it amusing.

A party of factory workers had decided to book a coach for a trip to see Blackpool's famous illuminations. As they were getting into the coach at dusk they were asked by a youth where they were going.

On being told that they were off to see the lights, he exclaimed, "Fancy going at this time — it'll be too dark to see owt when you get there!"

THE FRIENDSHIP BOOK

IT isn't always those who talk the most who have the most to say, if you understand my meaning.

I was invited to a family party recently to celebrate the engagement of Karen and Peter, and Karen's grandfather was the one who had been asked to propose the toast to the happy couple. Now Fred is very quiet, but he usually has a few words of wisdom ready for such an occasion. After a brief congratulation speech, he came out with this little pearl:

A good woman inspires a man,
A brilliant woman interests him,
A beautiful woman fascinates him,
But it's the sympathetic woman who keeps him.

It's a truth that many will already have experienced!

JANET, one of our old neighbours, is a Sunday School teacher and she calls in occasionally on her way home.

"I had a job not to laugh today," she recounted on one occasion. "I'd been telling the class about Adam and Eve and the Garden of Eden, and gave out paper and crayons so they could draw a picture. I could see that one little boy had done a lovely one with grass and flowers, the tree and the apple and the serpent, but right across the middle was a road and a red car with three people in it."

"Why have you put a car in your picture, Thomas?" I asked.

Thomas looked surprised. "It had to be there, Miss," he explained. "It's God driving Adam and Eve out of the garden."

THE FRIENDSHIP BOOK

ON a nature walk, watching sheep munching grass, a class of primary pupils was told by their teacher to notice just one thing about the animals, and then write about it back at school.

An abundance of observations reached her when marking the exercise, but one in particular made her think:

"The sheep never look up when they are eating, so they don't look where they are going and could easily go the wrong way and get lost," James had written.

There's truth in this for all of us. How easy it is to take too narrow a view, not taking time to look around and thus missing out on the many wonders of everyday life.

The familiar quotation springs to mind: What is this life, if full of care, we have no time to stand and stare?

FOR the first time ever we have successfully grown a begonia in our garden. We planted it in an ornamental pot and watched every stage of its progress with great interest.

It seemed to be in tight bud for many days, and we despaired of the petals ever opening. The sun shone warmly and conditions were ideal, but still the bud remained obstinately closed.

Then it burst into full bloom — a myriad scarlet petals in a flower six inches across, a constant source of pleasure to us each time we ventured out into the garden.

There is a time and season for all things in our lives and often events cannot be hurried. Like the begonia, when the conditions are right, our hopes will blossom.

THE FRIENDSHIP BOOK

A CLERICAL gentleman, staying in a country house, was descending the stairs on his way to breakfast one morning and was gratified to hear the words of the hymn, "Onward, Christian Soldiers" coming loud and clear from the kitchen.

He peeped round the door and congratulated the cook on her piety.

"Oh," she blushed, "I always cook my eggs this way. If I put the egg into boiling water and sing all five verses and the chorus, they are just right when I get to the Amen. If they want the eggs soft I just sing three verses!"

A practical lesson in the value of churchgoing.

A ND, behold, I send the promise of my Father upon you; but tarry ye in the city of Jerusalem, until ye be endued with power from on high.

Luke 24:49

UPS AND DOWNS

W HEN you least expect it,
Something good will come your way,
Might only be a small thing,
But enough to make your day.
Enough to make you want to smile,
And shout out loud "Hooray!"
Thank you, God, for all the "Ups",
And for keeping "Downs" at bay.

Phyllis Ellison.

TUESDAY—JULY 18.

THE writer Arthur Mee, who founded the "Children's Encyclopaedia" and the "Children's Newspaper", tells how he used to walk to work, each day passing a row of drab, little houses. They were built of red brick, with slate roofs, and each had its strip of garden.

In every case, this was uncultivated, so that the whole impression was one of ugliness and neglect.

One day, the man who lived in the end house took a spade and began to dig his patch. Then he got busy with packets of seed, and before long young plants started to appear. By the start of Summer the little plot of ground was a joy to behold with a profusion of colour.

The following year, his next-door neighbour made a similar start to *his* plot — and in a year or two all the previously neglected plots had been transformed into attractive gardens.

It all began with one man who made up his mind to make his own little patch into something lovely and worth looking at.

WEDNESDAY—JULY 19.

IN a neighbour's garden were Livingstone Daisies, those bright little flowers with pink, red or yellow petals. "These are lovely, Bill," I remarked.

"Yes," he agreed. "I hope I'm never like one, though."

I looked at him.

"Well," he said, "they're open now, because the sun's shining. As soon as the sky turns grey or it gets dark, they will close up and you won't see them again till the sun's back. You can't live like that!"

Indeed you can't.

THE FRIENDSHIP BOOK

I SUPPOSE most of us grow more forgetful as we get older. An amusing story is told of an earnest young minister who was visiting an eventide home for the first time. Surveying a roomful of elderly people he said solemnly, "I hope you are all giving a lot of thought to the hereafter."

A voice piped up: "Yes, I do! I often go up to my room or out to the garden and then start asking myself, 'Now, what am I here after?' "

"I SEE you have a couple of saints in your garden," my neighbour Bill called to me as he passed.

"I wasn't aware of it," I said.

"Look over there!" he replied, pointing at two tall sunflowers by the wall. "They got the name of being saints because they always turn towards the light."

An example to us all.

I CHUCKLED when I read the story of Dr Benjamin Jowett, one-time Master of Balliol College, Oxford.

One day a student came to his rooms and asked if he could be excused attendance at chapel. The reason he gave was that his faith was that of a sun-worshipper.

Dr Jowett showed no sign of surprise, and gave the student leave of absence from chapel. The youth went away smiling.

Next morning at 6 o'clock, the college scout knocked on the student's door and announced, "The Master's compliments, sir, the sun has just risen."

SUNDAY—JULY 23.

THY dead men shall live, together with my dead body shall they arise. Awake and sing, ye that dwell in dust; for thy dew is as the dew of herbs, and the earth shall cast out the dead.

Isaiah 26:19

MONDAY—JULY 24.

I LIKE the contrast between two verses penned many years ago by Louise W. Bunce.

"The world is full of evil," said the first,
And with denunciations fierce and long
He showed his fellows how on them sin-cursed,
Heaven's wrath would venge itself for every wrong.
Yet — they passed on unheeding.

"The world grows better," so the second said,
"Yet still needs help and comfort from the strong";
And showed his fellows, by his faith, love-fed,
How potent virtue is to right the wrong;
While throngs obeyed his leading.

TUESDAY—JULY 25.

WHEN we went to visit our old friend Mary she led us into her hall to show us the smoke alarm she'd bought.

"I think you are very wise to have one of those, Mary," I said. "It will give you extra peace of mind."

"Yes, I may be very thankful I have a smoke alarm one day. If that day doesn't come, I shall be very thankful that I don't *need* to be thankful."

It was a quaint way of putting it, but I knew exactly what she meant!

THE FRIENDSHIP BOOK

JULIA CARNEY was a schoolteacher in the USA and I am certain she was a very good one, for a poem she wrote contains this charming thought:

Little deeds of kindness, little words of love,
Help to make earth happy, like the heaven above.

YOU often see boxes of old postcards in secondhand shops. My friend Maurice sometimes buys one or two, and he often shows me his collection.

"There are photographs of towns and villages as I knew them when I was a lad, and they bring back lovely memories. Look at that one, for instance. I remember that little shop well!"

He likes to read the messages on the backs, too: "Having a grand holiday. The weather's superb", or "This is a beautiful spot. We're enjoying a picnic at the spot marked X".

Maurice has no idea who sent the cards — they're usually just signed with a Christian name — but he is sure that the senders of long ago would not mind if, now and again, he shares a little of the happiness they felt on these distant golden days.

A LITTLE boy who lived in London went to a farm for the first time. When he came back he was asked if he had enjoyed it and if he had seen anything special.

Yes, he said, he had seen something rather special. He saw a big pig and a lot of little pigs were trying to blow it up.

SUMMER COOL

THE FRIENDSHIP BOOK

OF all the customs we observe, handshaking is surely one of the most revealing. There is the dutiful handshake — just a brief touch, impersonal, meaningless. There is the complete opposite — the hearty, no-nonsense handshake — taking no account of the possible fact that the other hand may be racked with rheumatism!

Then there is the icy, stiff handshake that makes me think that Jack Frost reigns in the heart of the shaker, while there is the handshake which makes me feel the person is taking a liberty. Then there is the one which has sunbeams in it, one which gives you a warm glow, coming from a sincere and friendly heart.

Thinking on the matter has made me wonder what impression *my* handshake makes on others. Yes, I really must try to put more sunbeams into my grasp — it might save someone from frostbite.

FOR ye know the grace of our Lord Jesus Christ, that, though he was rich, yet for your sakes he became poor, that ye through his poverty might be rich.

Corinthians II 8:9

TIMES change, but in the little things, people remain the same. I think we must all recognise the simple truth expressed in this verse written by the poet William Cowper born in 1731:

For 'tis a truth well known to most,
That whatsoever thing is lost,
We seek it, ere it come to light,
In every cranny but the right!

AUGUST

TUESDAY—AUGUST 1.

I LIKE the story I heard about the two small boys who were watching bees in the garden one Summer's afternoon.

"Did you know that the bees are our friends?" asked the first little boy. "In the Summer they collect pollen from the flowers and take it back to the hive to make into honey."

"That's right," said the second boy, "and in the Winter they stay at home and put it into little pots for us to buy at the shop."

WEDNESDAY—AUGUST 2.

GEORGE is a quiet, sensitive man. When he returns from holiday it is always an unusual wild flower that he brings back as a memento, for his collection.

He is now an extremely sprightly 85-year-old, and will remark on a raindrop sparkling in the sunshine or the beauty of a flower slowly opening at dawn — he sees the things in life that many of us don't seem to notice at all.

The Lady of the House likes to chat with him as they walk around his garden. His hobby now is to photograph the small gardens round about that he has known for years. "Each day I watch for something new or unusual in these gardens," he says, "and I always find something that I've missed before."

George has never been famous or important, but to those who know him, he shines in his own very special way. He is the sort of person who creates a little bit of Heaven here on earth.

THE FRIENDSHIP BOOK

NOBODY can be in doubt when they hear the familiar shouts, squeals, and roar of the machinery — yes, it's the fun fair, in particular the mighty roller coaster with its inimitably bumpy and thrilling ride.

It's not a trip to be taken alone. You need a strong companion by your side, someone to cling to, to clutch frantically when that long, perilous drop begins, and someone to laugh with when the car climbs up safely again. Passengers go up and down, never quite knowing what is around the next bend.

It's rather like marriage, in fact, isn't it?

COFFEE MORNING

SOME cakes, please, for the cake stall
  And gifts for the tombola,
A pack of biscuits, tins of fruit,
Or cans of fizzy cola.
We always have white elephants
But we try to be discreet,
The things that we find ugly
To someone are a treat.

There's lots of friendly chatter,
Some gossip — nothing spiteful,
The cheerful clink of cups and spoons,
The coffee smells delightful.
Please come along at ten o'clock,
But just a word of warning:
Make sure there's money in your purse,
Enjoy our coffee morning!

                                    Iris Hesselden.

THE FRIENDSHIP BOOK

THE Lady of the House and I love to visit great buildings — cathedrals, mansions, castles. Very often, when we talk about it afterwards, we find that what impressed us most was not the splendid architecture, the fine furnishings or paintings. No, it's something more simple than any of these. It's the way the sun was shining through the windows, throwing great golden rays across the floors and walls.

Robert Frost, the American poet, described light as "God's eldest daughter" and praised it as one of the principal beauties of any great building.

All that man has to do is provide the windows for the light to shine through. Then He does the rest!

AND God made two great lights; the greater light to rule the day, and the lesser light to rule the night: he made the stars also.

Genesis 1:16

HAVE you heard of the American prison governor who spent a week in one of his own cells? No, he had done nothing wrong, but he did not feel he could understand his prisoners' problems until he had endured their kind of life. Throughout his stay he insisted that the warders treated him in exactly the same way as the others.

Of course, we can't all take such a drastic step, but we *can* all make an effort to think ourselves into other people's shoes, imagining how they feel and so coming to understand their problems and fears. Then, like the governor, we can set about giving the helping hand that is needed.

THE FRIENDSHIP BOOK

A YOUNG friend sent me this prayer and asked me to pass it on, which I now gladly do:

Just a little word of kindness,
Just a little word of love,
Just a little smile of tenderness,
Are all blessings from above.

Just a little thought of comfort,
Just a token that you care,
Just a little gesture of sympathy,
May be answer to a prayer.

Just a little smile of happiness,
Just a little song of peace,
Just a word of praise at eventide,
Will give the soul release.

For the little bit of kindness,
And the little bit of care,
The little bit of tenderness,
Are the essence of a prayer.

CHILDREN have a happy knack of translating difficult concepts into facts they can readily grasp. On one occasion a teacher was taking an outdoor class in the Yorkshire countryside, explaining its geology and ancient history.

"Can you imagine," he asked, "that Malhamdale was once a sea and there were fishes swimming where you are standing now?"

"I know, sir," called out one small boy, "and to prove it I've just found a sardine tin."

THE FRIENDSHIP BOOK

H ERE'S your sweet lavender,
Sixteen sprigs a penny,
Which you will find, my ladies,
Will smell as sweet as any.

So goes one of the old London street cries. Lots of people refer to it as Old English lavender, but it is really a Mediterranean plant. The Romans brought it to Britain more than 2,000 years ago to perfume the water in the baths that were so important to them. That is how it got its name — from the Latin *lavo*, "I wash".

If you look round a garden on a warm Summer's day, you will notice that the lavender bushes are always covered with bees busy collecting the nectar, and the honey produced from it is particularly delicious. The monks grew this plant, both for the bees and also for all sorts of medicinal purposes — it used to be said that "flowers of lavender comfort the braines very well."

As in olden days, these flowers are still dried to use in lavender bags or pot pourri to add fragrance to our homes, or distilled to produce lavender oil. What a lot we owe to these Romans of old!

C H. SPURGEON once wrote: "When I went to school, we drew such things as houses, horses and trees, and used to write the word 'house' under the picture of the house, and the word 'horse' under the picture of the horse. Otherwise some people might have mistaken the house for a horse! So there are some people who should wear a label around their necks to show they are Christians or else we might mistake them for sinners."

THE FRIENDSHIP BOOK

I HAVE just come across this anonymous little thought which I'd like to pass on today:

"Laughter is like music that lingers in the heart; and when its melody is heard the ills of life depart." So remember — a smile always adds to our face value.

THIS is my commandment, That ye love one another, as I have loved you. Greater love hath no man than this, that a man lay down his life for his friends.

John 15:12-13

IF only I were perfect,
I would gracefully accept
The envy of all people
Who are lazy and inept.

If only I were perfect,
I'd spread the news around,
And hope that bold exponents
Of my message could be found.

If only I were perfect,
I would clearly understand
The problems that beset the world,
And thereby take command.

If only I were perfect . . .
But then Life would be no fun,
For day by day, it's safe to say,
I'd be the only one!

J.M. Robertson

GUARDIAN OF THE NIGHT

THE FRIENDSHIP BOOK

*ALL negative thoughts I've
decided must go,*
I'll try to say, "Yes" when I want to say, "No."
I won't say, "I can't," but, "I can only try,"
*And accept things that happen — not keep
asking why.*

I'll make time for hobbies and brighten my day,
And not let my problems affect what I say,
*There are many folk homeless, sad, hungry,
in pain,*
I am blessed with so much, I'll not grumble again.

Today will be good for I'm filled now with hope,
With God's love inside me, I know I can cope,
No moanings or groanings, no sighing, no dread,
My positive thoughts are all there instead.

Chrissy Greenslade.

THE Maoris of New Zealand are a proud people with many fine traditions. My favourite story relates to the time when there was skirmishing and bloodshed between them and some of the early settlers.

Some settlers were under siege in an encampment and food was running low. On learning this, the Maoris sent in fresh supplies with the message: "We do not fight starving men."

The outcome of the siege is not recorded, but that generous action illustrates how, even in war, honour and compassion can still prevail. You might even say — with enemies like these, who needs friends?

THE FRIENDSHIP BOOK

I SUPPOSE most of us take our feet for granted — that is, until we hurt one of them. Then we realise how much we need them both. I have been seeing my own feet in a new light since I talked recently with an elderly chiropodist.

"The human feet," he said to me, "start off as two beautiful instruments. They give perfect balance to the body and they are designed so that they grip the ground as we walk. Yet what do people do with them? Cram them into ill-fitting boots and shoes so that they lose their natural grace and become clumsy and misshapen. It's a crime!"

It's the same with a whole number of God's gifts, isn't it? Our hands, our eyes, our brains: if we neglect or abuse them, they don't work the way they should, the way He intended.

DURING the Second World War the Bishop of Singapore, Leonard Wilson, was captured by the Japanese, put in a crowded prison and tortured. His captors asked him why he did not curse them, and he replied that he was a follower of Jesus Christ who taught us that we are brothers.

This was very difficult because the torture inflicted was dreadful. He tried hard not to hate his captors, and gradually found a way to achieve this. He later said that he imagined them as they were when they were children. "It is hard to hate little children," he said.

Sometimes it is very difficult not to be angry. To succeed, like Leonard Wilson, we need measureless self-control and patience — and to know how to forgive.

THE FRIENDSHIP BOOK

I HAVE a friend in Yorkshire whose great-grandfather was a lamplighter. He once told me this family story.

He said that his great-grandfather always took his dog Gyp with him on his rounds, and he had done this since the dog was a tiny puppy. One damp, foggy night, however, he found that Gyp was not following him. He called and whistled without result, then finally decided to go back to look for him. He found him sitting beside a lamp-post where the lamp had not been lit.

Gyp knew the job every bit as well as his master did, and meant to do his part of it properly. It just goes to show how valuable and conscientious our animal companions can be — our best friends indeed.

O GIVE thanks unto the Lord, for he is good: for his mercy endureth for ever.

Chronicles I 16:34

CIRCLE OF LOVE

STILL it gives me pleasure,
  As I look upon my hand,
It isn't very modern,
    Just a plain gold band.
It didn't cost a fortune,
    But all we had that day,
We think it was a bargain,
    It brought happiness our way.

Phyllis Ellison.

THE FRIENDSHIP BOOK

I CAN'T think of many occasions when I am pleased to be held up at traffic lights. The exception is when I have to stop outside a nearby church and have the chance of reading the Wayside Pulpit notice. Over the years I have added quite a lot of homilies to my collection. Here are some you might like to share today:

The tests of life are the tests of character.

When you count the gifts of God you never stop calculating.

Prayer — not just for emergencies only.

Prayer reaches the parts nothing else can reach.

Seven days without prayer makes one weak.

Prayers travel faster when said in unison.

Come to Church next Sunday and avoid the Christmas rush.

DAVE and Len retired the same month. Dave immediately started to learn to play golf, something he's always wanted to do. He has also joined a couple of committees and helps in a charity shop. He's always on the go.

Len just wants to take things easy. He goes to the shop for his paper in the morning and sits in the house most of the day.

You'll not be surprised to hear that Dave looks fit and happy. He has made a host of new friends. Len has been looking bored and down in the mouth. He's getting overweight. However, I think there's hope for him. Why? Well, I saw Dave having a long chat with him in the street yesterday and it finished with Len looking up dates in his diary . . .

THE FRIENDSHIP BOOK

ALFRED WAINWRIGHT loved walking and was never happier than when he was climbing in the mountains of the Lake District. He was a solitary man, and if you met him he was nearly always alone. "The hills are my friends," he would say.

As he walked along, he would draw maps and sketches, and when he went home he wrote and illustrated beautiful and lively books about the journeys he had made.

When Alfred Wainwright died, he had not only the hills as his friends, but countless readers — many, perhaps, who would never have the opportunity to explore the Lake District, but who had shared his adventures with him through his books.

This blunt, but kind and gifted gentleman left behind a legacy of love.

IN our local art-class we are fortunate to have a tutor who is both sensitive and enthusiastic. One afternoon he was arranging a still-life piece for us and said, "Note the varying textures, ladies and gentlemen," pointing to the pottery vase, the bowl of fruit and the flowers. "I think we'll have more light," he added. "I'll move the curtain a little to the left; we must always put our models in the best light if we want to draw them correctly. Yes, that's better, now you can see the highlights, and the shadow. Now you can begin drawing."

What an apt comment on our relationships with our fellow men! If we could only see the other person in their best light at all times, unexpected virtues, undreamed of highlights would appear. It's all a matter of perspective, isn't it?

THE FRIENDSHIP BOOK

SATURDAY—AUGUST 26.

GOOD health is a wonderful advantage, of course, but it is not an essential passport to success. If we consider writers, for instance, Robert Louis Stevenson was a chronic invalid most of his life, Charles Dickens was plagued with illness, while the Brontë sisters were delicate from birth.

It's the spirit that counts. It can rise above all adversity. It did it for them. It can do it for you.

SUNDAY—AUGUST 27.

AND ye shall take you on the first day the boughs of goodly trees, branches of palm trees, and the boughs of thick trees, and willows of the brook; and ye shall rejoice before the Lord your God seven days.

Leviticus 23:40

MONDAY—AUGUST 28.

MY young friend James recently became one of the world's 14 million Scouts and I was proud to be invited along to the ceremony.

Amongst other things, I learned the reason why Scouts, Cub Scouts, Guides and Brownies shake hands with their left hand. Apparently Baden-Powell, founder of the Scout movement, saw this done by natives when he was serving in the army in Africa. It was a sign of trust between them, for they had to lay down their shields and leave themselves unprotected as they greeted each other.

Baden-Powell adopted the practice as one of the ideals he wished to incorporate in the world-wide brotherhood of Scouting. It is still in force almost 90 years on!

THE FRIENDSHIP BOOK

BE A FRIEND

*W*E may not have much time to spare
  To pause along the way,
But what a difference we could make
  To someone's lonely day!
A cheerful voice, a kindly chat,
  The thoughts that understand —
These simple things that make us glad
  To lend a helping hand.

Elizabeth Gozney.

IN the United States, a woman fell out of a second-floor window, and landed in a slow-moving rubbish lorry. Half-buried, she tried without success to attract the driver's attention.

A foreign diplomat passing her on the pavement exclaimed, "Another example of how wasteful Americans are! That woman looks like she's good for at least another 10 years."

A true story? Well, it's a good one, anyway!

I NEVER tire hearing of Mother Teresa and the outstanding work carried out for the needy folk of Calcutta.

I came across another of her thought-provoking epigrams recently and would like to share it with you today:

"It's not how much you do — it's how much love you put into the doing."

SEPTEMBER

EARLY MORNING

A GLIMPSE through my window,
As the mist swirls away,
Shows me the promise,
Of another fine day.
How shall I spend it?
Soon I shall see,
First, thank you, Lord,
For giving it me.

Phyllis Ellison.

WHEN I was young the golden fields of waving grain were often sprinkled with the bright red of wild poppies. What a lovely sight they were, and they flourished Autumn after Autumn.

Then came chemical sprays and the poppies in our neighbourhood all but disappeared. We thought they had gone for ever, but, miracle of miracles, they popped up again in different parts of the county.

How did it happen? Well, though I'm told it's because not so many sprays are being used now, the real miracle is this: the seeds lingered in the ground year after year until conditions once again allowed them to germinate.

Isn't it wonderful to think of those tiny seeds lying waiting in the darkness of the soil until the chance came again to spread their flowers across the land?

What a triumph for beauty!

STILL SUMMER

THE FRIENDSHIP BOOK

HOLD fast the form of sound words, which thou hast heard of me, in faith and love which is in Christ Jesus.

Timothy II 1:13

THE choir had been practising hard for their part in the Saturday evening concert in the village hall. Unfortunately, the compere hesitated just a fraction too long when he made his announcement:

"Now, ladies and gentlemen, the choir are ready with their contribution . . . 'Never Mind' . . ."

Not quite what he intended to say, I'm sure!

ALL right, I admit it — many prayers sound very old-fashioned. Perhaps that's why I rather like this one, written for you and me today:

I leave aside my shoes — my ambitions,
undo my watch — my timetable,
take off my glasses — my views,
unclip my pen — my work,
put down my keys — my security,
to be alone with You, the only true God.

After being with You,
I take up my shoes to walk in Your ways,
Strap on my watch to live in Your time,
Put on my glasses to look at Your world,
Clip on my pen to write up Your thoughts,
Pick up my keys to open Your doors.

Anon.

THE FRIENDSHIP BOOK

I CAN think of no lovelier season than harvest time, particularly for those who live in a rural area or who have a productive garden. There can be few things more satisfying than eating something you have grown yourself — fresh lettuces, crisp runner beans and ripe tomatoes — or picking a glorious-coloured bunch of dahlias.

Wherever we live, we may be grateful for yet another harvest safely home, for those who have worked on the land to bring it about, and for the providence of God in giving us our daily bread:

"For it is fed and watered by God's Almighty Hand."

This prayer (author unknown) expresses harvest thoughts beautifully:

For rosy apples, juicy plums,
And yellow pears so sweet,
For hips and haws on bush and hedge,
And flowers at our feet;
For ears of corn all ripe and dry,
And coloured leaves on trees,
We thank you, Heavenly Father God,
For such good gifts as these.

WHEN Christopher Columbus set out on his historical voyage of discovery, he didn't know where he was going when he set off, he didn't know where he was when he got there, and when he'd been there, he didn't even know where he'd been — but he'd found a great new world in the process.

So when things perplex or bother you, and you don't know which way to go . . . then remember Christopher Columbus.

THE FRIENDSHIP BOOK

IT was a wet day and the artist could not get out into the fields to paint as he usually did. He looked around him and his eyes fell upon a vase of flowers. Well, it would be better than nothing . . .

Thus Vincent Van Gogh painted "The Sunflowers", one of the world's most famous pictures. He was to execute many projects that were much more ambitious, but this study of yellow blooms in a vase has captured hearts worldwide.

It will still be loved for its simplicity long after the works of pretentious "fashionable" artists are forgotten.

WHO'S the one who'll understand,
When I'm worried takes my hand,
Tells me, "Mum, you're looking grand"—
My daughter.

Who is it that always seems to know
When I'm blue and feeling low,
Then says, "Mum, I love you so"—
My daughter.

Who can chatter on no end,
Sometimes drives me round the bend,
But will always be my friend—
My daughter.

Who can all the world beguile,
With the sweetness of her smile
Who makes everything worthwhile—
My daughter.

Jean Forrest.

JUST CHATTING

THE FRIENDSHIP BOOK

BUT the fruit of the Spirit is love, joy, peace, longsuffering, gentleness, goodness, faith, Meekness, temperance: against such there is no law.

Galatians 5:22-23

SUNDAY—SEPTEMBER 11.

WALKING our dog in a nearby country lane not long ago, I met two small children. They'd been picking brambles, and were in a thoroughly bedraggled and scratched state.

"Oh, my, your hands and arms must be sore!" I said sympathetically.

"They are a bit," grinned young Mike, "but just look at what we've picked! Mum loves brambles."

Well, there's an example of the power of love if ever there was one!

TUESDAY—SEPTEMBER 12.

IT was good to see my old friend Mary again. As we sat together in her cosy sitting-room, she handed me her "special book," the one in which she copies down items, verses and thoughts that she finds particularly helpful or comforting.

"You might like this for your 'Friendship Book', Francis," she said, showing me her latest entry:

I thank God for the mountains
And I thank Him for the valleys,
I thank Him for the storms He brought me through,
For if I'd never had a problem
I wouldn't know that He could solve them,
I'd never know what faith in God could do.

It's seldom I come away from Mary without something new to ponder over.

THE FRIENDSHIP BOOK

HAVE you heard of the poet Janet Hamilton? I won't be surprised if you haven't for she is almost forgotten today. Yet she deserves to be remembered, not just for her poems, but for her remarkable spirit.

Born in Lanarkshire in 1795 she could read by the age of five, but did not learn to write until she was 54. She was married at 13, had ten children and always lived in straitened circumstances. Yet this woman turned out poetry in Scots and English which was admired by leading figures of the day.

She wrote mostly about the ordinary things around her, and she often attacked drink which destroyed so many lives at that time. Through her poems she encouraged others to strive to better themselves through education and hard work.

In one poem, after describing her lowly upbringing she wrote:

Yet not low my aspirations:
  High and strong my soul's desire
To assist my toiling brothers
  Upwards, onwards to aspire.

FORMER Senator Dwight W. Morrow searched in vain to find his railway ticket on a train leaving New York.

"I must find it!" he muttered.

Then the railway official, who stood waiting beside him, said, "Don't worry about it, Mr Morrow. We know you had a ticket. Just post it when you find it."

"That's not what's troubling me," replied Morrow. "I need to find it to know where I'm going!"

THE FRIENDSHIP BOOK

ANGLERS may be accused at times of exaggerating the size of their catches, and stories of the "one that got away" have been met with disbelief since fishing began. That's why I can't help feeling for the angler who prayed:

Give me, O Lord, to catch a fish
   So large that even I
In boasting of it afterwards
   Shall have no need to lie.

I am reminded that on a village churchyard grave in Devon are to be found the words of yet another angler's prayer:

God grant that I may fish until my dying day,
And when it comes to my last cast, I humbly pray,
When in the Lord's safe landing net I'm peacefully
   asleep
That in His mercy I be judged good enough to
   keep.

MICHAEL, a retired engineer, was asked if he would write a guide for an "industrial trail" in his town, to be used by local schools. It proved to be an interesting project, not just for himself, but for others, too — he felt like a seasoned author when he came to compile the acknowledgements! Artists, staff at the records office and library, and elderly people who could remember working in the factories years ago had all helped.

When the book was published, Michael found how many new friends he had made and also realised how many things there are in life which cannot be done on your own. When we work together great success can be achieved.

THE FRIENDSHIP BOOK

LET your heart therefore be perfect with the Lord our God, to walk in his statutes, and to keep his commandments, as at this day.

Kings I 8:61

I LIKE this story I heard about a small boy who was taken to church by his father.

He watched the collection plate being passed round with great interest. When it reached them and he saw his father putting his hand in his pocket, the little lad whispered, "Daddy, Daddy, you don't need to pay for me. I'm only three!"

MRS I. J. STEVENSON of Allestree, Derby, sent me a number of verses she has collected over the years. She tells me they have helped her enormously along life's journey and I can well understand why. Here is one of them:

The best is never over,
*   The best has never gone,*
There's always something lovely
*   to keep you struggling on;*
There's always compensation
*   For every cross you bear,*
A secret consolation
*   Hidden well somewhere.*
Ends are new beginnings
*   As one day you will see;*
The best is never over,
*   The best is yet to be.*

THE FRIENDSHIP BOOK

ARE you superstitious? I'm not really, but I don't usually walk under ladders, all the same — even when there isn't a workman at the top precariously balancing a paint pot or a bucket of water.

Ladders come in various types. There is the rope ladder which folds up and would have been used in battle in earlier times when there was a city wall or castle wall to be climbed.

Fish ladders are used to help salmon when they are coming in from the sea to begin their breeding cycle. These ladders enable them to reach higher levels in rivers.

Firemen use turntable ladders to fight fires, and the ladders are vital in rescuing trapped people.

My first childhood recollection of ladders was in the board game of Snakes and Ladders which youngsters still play today.

However, the ladder I like the best is referred to in the Old Testament. Jacob in a dream saw a ladder set up on earth and the top of it reached to Heaven with angels ascending and descending.

READING is, and always has been, a favourite pastime of mine. I enjoy the theatre, and a good many programmes on television and radio, but the printed word has its unique charms. You can imagine, then, how my heart warmed when I read these words written by the great novelist Anthony Trollope:

"Love of books is your pass to the greatest, the purest, and the most perfect pleasure that God has prepared for His creatures. It lasts when all other recreations are gone. It will make your hours pleasant to you as long as you live."

FRIDAY—SEPTEMBER 22.

WHAT a difference a letter — or the absence of one — makes; and this time I don't mean the kind you send through the post.

Members of a Dundee congregation were surprised to read the following question in their monthly news-sheet:

"If your neighbours and fiends were to come to our church, would they feel welcome?"

SATURDAY—SEPTEMBER 23.

WE can't underestimate the power of prayer, or the comfort it can bring. Here is an anonymous poem which says it all:

> *Just close your eyes*
> *   And open your heart*
> *And feel your worries*
> *   And cares depart,*
> *Just yield yourself*
> *   To the Father above*
> *And let Him hold you*
> *   Secure in his love.*
> *For life on earth*
> *   Grows more involved*
> *With endless problems*
> *   That can't be solved.*
>
> *So when you are tired,*
> *   Discouraged and blue,*
> *There's only one door*
> *   That is open to you,*
> *And that is the door to*
> *   The House of Prayer,*
> *You'll find God waiting*
> *   To meet you there.*

THE FRIENDSHIP BOOK

AND it shall be said in that day, Lo, this is our God; we have waited for him, and he will save us; this is the Lord, we have waited for him, we will be glad and rejoice in his salvation.

Isaiah 25:9

"I'VE been having trouble with rheumatism today, Mr Gay," said young Billy when I met him on the way home from school.

"I'm very sorry to hear that, Billy," I said. "You're rather young to have rheumatism."

"Oh, it's not that, Mr Gay," said Billy with a grin. "It's just that I was having trouble spelling it!"

I HAVE been reading some good advice about how to live in harmony with our neighbours. Here are some thoughts I'd like to share with you:

"Never tell your neighbours to wait until tomorrow if you can help now."

"Don't plan anything that will hurt your neighbours; they live beside you, trusting you."

"If you and your neighbours have a difference of opinion, settle it between yourselves and do not reveal any secrets."

"Don't visit your neighbours too often; they may get tired of you and come to hate you."

"Neighbours nearby can help you more than a brother who is far away."

Were these wise words from the pen of a modern psychologist or the pages of a women's magazine? No, they were from the Book of Proverbs in the Bible written about 2,800 years ago!

THE FRIENDSHIP BOOK

ONE of the finest of human virtues is faithfulness. It's not surprising that, in Scotland, Heaven used to be known as "The land o' the leal (or faithful)".

A land filled with faithful people would be a wonderful place indeed.

I USED to visit an aunt who lived not far away in a small village. On my way there, I would pass a house with a large garden, but was disgusted to see that all the flowers were plastic ones! "How very lazy the inhabitants must be," I thought. "Too idle to plant proper flowers."

When, however, I remarked on this to my aunt she told another story. Apparently the elderly couple there had been keen gardeners and the lady was passionately fond of flowers. She had very poor eyesight, suffered badly from arthritis, and spent many hours looking out of her window.

Her husband, equally arthritic and suffering from a heart complaint, couldn't bear to see her disappointed from the lack of flowers in the garden, so he laboriously planted the plastic ones as soon as their seasons came round and thought, with her poor sight, his wife would think they were real!

However, the lady confided in Auntie that she knew they were *not* real flowers. "You won't tell Bill, will you? I wouldn't like to disappoint him after all the hard work he has put in!"

I was quite ashamed of my initial uncharitable thoughts and remembered what my grandmother used to say: "You can't always judge the jam by the label on the jar."

THE FRIENDSHIP BOOK

TO any reader who today is finding the road of life rough, I say — keep going. Remember, it takes a little rain as well as sun to make a rainbow.

MOTHERING SUNDAY is one of our long-established family celebrations and Father's Day has come to stay, too, but did you know that the last Saturday in September is Grandparents' Day?

It was started in 1990 by Age Concern because of the fear that through social mobility, increase in divorce and the tendency of young people to move away from home at an earlier age, grandparents and their grandchildren were in danger of losing that very special relationship between the young and the old.

It is the special role of grandparents to be more indulgent than a parent, to have time to listen, to babysit and to share confidences; while nearly every grandparent I meet claims that having grandchildren brings a new lease of life.

Grandparents' Day is not without its commercial side, of course, and shops are offering gifts, cards and flowers, but if it results in families being brought closer together, then I am all in favour.

I am reminded of a story told by Dr William Barclay. A grandfather and his small grandson were walking on the beach when they met another elderly gentleman. He was full of grumbles and to crown it all, he had a touch of sunstroke. The little boy had been listening to the conversation, but didn't get it quite right. As they parted he put his small hand into the larger one and gave it a squeeze, saying:

"Grandpa, I hope *you* never catch a sunset."

So, on this newest of family days, I raise my hat to all grandparents — and to the benefits it brings.

OCTOBER

<u>SUNDAY—OCTOBER 1.</u>

THE grace of the Lord Jesus Christ, and the love of God, and the communion of the Holy Ghost, be with you all. Amen.

Corinthians II 13:14

<u>MONDAY—OCTOBER 2.</u>

BETTINA SELBY has travelled through many countries on her bicycle and has written books describing her experiences.

Once, when a guide was leading her through an African town rife with poverty, they came on a little boy begging in the street. On impulse Bettina placed in his hands her lunch of bread and tomatoes.

The boy's eyes were large with gratitude as he took it and she expected that he would start to eat it right away. Instead, he ran over to another boy and gave him a share of the precious food.

Bettina was amazed, but the guide showed no surprise. "In Africa," he told her, "if one eats, all eat."

<u>TUESDAY—OCTOBER 3.</u>

WE'VE all met them — the people who have to let the whole world know how kind and generous they have been.

In Charles Dickens' novel "Bleak House", the wise John Jarndyce remarks that there are two kinds of charitable folk — those who do a little good, but make a great deal of noise about it, and those who do a great deal, quietly and without fuss.

I know which ones I would like to be counted amongst, don't you?

THE FRIENDSHIP BOOK

GLENDA MOORE, the Doncaster poet, wrote these delightful verses about her own special "Quiet Corner":

> *There's a corner in my garden,*
> *A cosy little nook,*
> *Where I often take my ease,*
> *To knit or read a book.*
>
> *I've contemplated patterns,*
> *On that seat beneath the tree,*
> *A blackbird's song, a clear blue sky,*
> *Or what to have for tea.*
>
> *I iron out knotty problems,*
> *Solve crosswords by the score,*
> *Darn old socks, check recipes,*
> *Chat to the girl next door.*
>
> *World affairs are quite forgotten,*
> *And time scurries on a-pace,*
> *When I'm lost in contemplation,*
> *In my little thinking place.*

A FRIEND sent me a bookmark some time ago, and it was to become a firm favourite of mine.

If I feel a little down I take the book I'm currently reading from the shelf and read these words on the marker:

"Life is a series of fresh starts and new beginnings."

How very true!

L

THE FRIENDSHIP BOOK

WHEN I was a small boy I liked to read about the cuckoo on the chimney pot in one of my story books.

All through the Summer the cuckoo had enjoyed being in the woodlands, but as the days got chillier he found a rooftop with a comfortable, warm chimney pot that he could snuggle up against. The other birds began flying off to warmer lands for the Winter and they called out, "Come along, cuckoo, it's getting cold. It's time for you to be flying off with us." However, the cuckoo replied that he was perfectly warm where he was and intended to stay there.

Then, one day, the people in the house went away for the weekend, the fires went out and the chimney pot grew cold. The cuckoo realised that Winter really was on the way and he had better make haste to join his friends in a warm country while there was still time.

This is only a story, but I think it has a message for us. If we are in a predicament and have friends whom we can trust, it is a good idea to listen to their advice, for they may know something that we don't!

A LITTLE girl who was waiting for a routine operation was terrified at the prospect of the unknown.

To keep her in good spirits, her parents promised her something she had wanted for a long time — a kitten.

In due course, the operation went very well, but as the anaesthetic was wearing off, the youngster was heard mumbling to herself, "This is a terrible way to get a cat!"

THE FRIENDSHIP BOOK

AND he said unto them, Go ye into all the world, and preach the gospel to every creature.

Mark 16:15

IF you think up some kindly word,
Or you've a joke that should be heard,
Some time to listen, time to smile,
Some deed to make the day worthwhile,
Share it with a friend.

Perhaps you've made a cake for tea,
Or find you have an hour that's free,
Some time to welcome, time to stay,
Some time to chase the blues away,
Share it with a friend.

If you would write a line or two,
Or send a postcard with a view,
Some time to ponder, time to greet,
Some word to make the day complete,
Share it with a friend.

Barbara Roper.

A HOLIDAYMAKER in the far west of Ireland went into a shop and asked for a newspaper.

The shopkeeper looked at him. "Is it yesterday's or today's you're wanting?"

"Today's, please."

"Oh, then you'll have to come back tomorrow."

GOLDEN WONDER

THE FRIENDSHIP BOOK

YOU can often tell people's characters from the expression on their faces; some folk positively radiate confidence and cheerfulness. This thought came to me as I read a story about an early President of the United States, Thomas Jefferson.

With a group of companions Jefferson was travelling cross-country on horseback. They came to a river in flood; it had overflowed its banks and the one bridge had been washed away. The party decided to force a crossing on horseback, though it would be difficult and dangerous through the rapid currents.

A man, part of another party, asked Jefferson if he would take him across on his horse. He agreed and the two men safely reached the other side. As they stood there, one of the group asked the stranger, "Why did you choose the President to carry you across?" This came as a shock to the man, who had no idea that he had so distinguished a rescuer.

"All I know," he said, "is that on some of your faces was written the answer 'No', and on some of them the answer 'Yes'. His was a 'Yes' face."

What a blessing it would be if we could all carry 'Yes' faces!

SEE the trust a little child
    Puts into your care,
All her precious world is safe,
    As long as you are there.
When she slips her hand in yours,
    And smiles replace the tears,
Know that it was you
    To whom she brought her childish fears.
                    Elizabeth Gozney.

THE FRIENDSHIP BOOK

LAST year, the Lady of the House and I received a welcome letter from friends living in another part of the country. They are busy people, working full time at demanding jobs, and they commute several miles daily.

We were therefore surprised to learn that they were both taking a college course to enable them to teach adults the basic skills of reading, writing and coping with figures. We thought it was a splendid idea. Those of us who are able to read, write and understand figures tend to take our knowledge very much for granted.

Our friends are both now qualified to teach on a voluntary basis and are looking forward to the new challenge. As they say, "It's nice to put a little of what we've taken out of life back into it again."

THESE lines by Professor William Barclay were shown to me by our friend Mary who likes to collect helpful thoughts and verses, and I am passing them on in the hope that there will be a useful message here for *you* today.

It is hunger which gives food its taste.
It is thirst which make cool, clear water taste like nectar.
It is tiredness which makes sleep a boon.
It is toil which makes rest a blessing.
It is loneliness which gives friendship its value.
It is the rain which gives sunshine its joy.
It is the dark night which gives the dawn its glory.
It is parting which makes meeting again a happy thing.

BUT thou, O Lord, art a God full of compassion, and gracious, longsuffering, and plenteous in mercy and truth.

Psalms 86:15

MONDAY—OCTOBER 16.

I HAVE come across another of those stories which show you can't always get the better of reputedly unworldly parsons. On one occasion a family of gypsies passing through the countryside had left a dead donkey in a village churchyard.

The perplexed vicar, not knowing what to do, reported the matter to the local council.

A facetious council official taking the call, commented, "I thought it was your duty, vicar, to bury the dead!"

"It is," replied the quick-thinking minister, "but I thought I should at least notify the relatives of the deceased first!"

TUESDAY—OCTOBER 17.

A CHILDHOOD delight is flying a kite. What happy, peaceful hours I enjoyed with that soaring paper bird! The kite itself might have reasoned: "I'm flying high and gracefully, despite that child down there hanging on to the string. Without that handicap I could float off to the moon."

Could it, though? Whenever I let go of the string the kite crashed, or became entangled in a tree.

Just like the kite, we need a tether to keep us sensibly grounded, but we also benefit by raising our eyes from the earthbound at least once a day. Spirits are made for soaring!

THE FRIENDSHIP BOOK

I LIKE the story of a Methodist group from the Wesley Guild, who had been visiting and entertaining at a Methodist Home For The Aged on the Isle of Wight.

As they were returning in an open-topped bus, they were singing happily, and the conductor gave them an unusual token of appreciation. He said, "You're like recycled teenagers!"

I have it on good authority that most of those Wesley Guilders were senior citizens — in fact, three in their late eighties!

It just goes to show what I've always known, that age is no barrier to enjoyment of life.

OF course it's nice to win at games, but does it matter all that much? The poet Grantland Rice didn't think so. Writing of the game of life, he said:

For when the one Great Scorer comes
To write against your name,
He marks — not that you won or lost —
But how you played the game.

SYLVIA is blessed with a family of three lively young sons.

One day, seven-year-old Christopher came home from school with the news that if she had another baby it would be Chinese! When asked to explain, he revealed that they had learned at school that every fourth baby born is Chinese!

THE FRIENDSHIP BOOK

"IT is often better not to see an insult than to attempt to avenge it."

This was the warning given by Seneca the Younger who died in AD 65, and the passing years have made it no less worthy of emulation.

From more modern times I came across this piece of advice: "A true friend will never take offence or harbour a grudge. Real love makes allowances, suspends judgment and withholds uncharitable comments."

Easier said than done perhaps, but I am sure it is worth the effort. For myself, I am resolved to follow the French proverb:

"Write injuries in sand — kindess in marble."

I HAVE surely built thee an house to dwell in, a settled place for thee to abide in for ever.

Kings I 8:13

DID you hear the story about the two old men who were fishing from a boat on a Highland loch?

Murdo bent over the side, and his false teeth fell out and disappeared into the water. "Oh, well," he decided, "I won't spoil Donald's day by telling him what's happened."

A few minutes later Donald gave a shout. "Murdo, I've got a bite!" He wound in his reel and there, on the hook, dangled the false teeth.

Before Murdo could say a word, the furious Donald grunted in disappointment, grabbed the teeth and flung them as far as he could back into the loch!

THE FRIENDSHIP BOOK

TUESDAY—OCTOBER 24.

DORIS CARTER of Winchester told me this amusing story about her grandfather's congregation. Most were farm workers, cowmen, shepherds and the occasional "gentleman farmer".

As her grandfather had other chapels he cared for, he was not able to visit every one each Sunday. So a member of the congregation took the service himself. On one occasion a burly farm labourer was preaching the "sermon".

He started by saying, "I'm just tillin' the ground, yer might say. Diggin' the furrows like, and getting the ground ready. Next week Pastor will be here and he will plant t'seed."

WEDNESDAY—OCTOBER 25.

TO annoy a Christian, an unbeliever once wrote on a wall in large letters: God Is Nowhere.

The Christian simply smiled and amended it: God Is Now Here.

THURSDAY—OCTOBER 26.

MY friend Joe was on his knees in his garden when I passed. No, he wasn't praying — he was pulling out weeds with his hands.

"Why don't you take the hoe to them, Joe?" I asked. "It would be a lot less work."

He looked at me. "Weeds are like bad habits," he said. "You've got to pull them right out by the roots. Leave anything of them and they'll soon grow again, worse than ever."

He held up a weed, root and all. "Look," he said. "That's the only way to treat a weed — or a bad habit."

It's not the first time I've found Joe's gardening tips are a philosophy of life as well!

THE FRIENDSHIP BOOK

RECENTLY I re-read a book by S.P.B. Mair, a traveller and gifted writer. In it he recalls memories of his 21st birthday and his official entry to man's estate.

He was a schoolteacher at the time, and that day he put in 17 hours of work, preparing for lessons, teaching during the day, superintending after-school activities, then marking exercises when he arrived home. I must confess it certainly wasn't the way I spent *my* 21st birthday!

However, Mair recalls his 21st birthday as by far the happiest day of his life. Why? He had so much to do that he had no time to think of himself. He felt that was the secret of happiness. He concluded, "The moment you have time to think of yourself, you are on the way to being miserable."

He's got a point, hasn't he?

AT this time of year I plant bulbs — dry objects which look not at all promising. As I drop each one into its hole, cover it with earth and smooth over the surface, I reflect that during the Winter those dried-up bulbs will remain in the ground, hidden and largely forgotten. The miracle of new growth will already have started, though, and next Spring, I'll be able to see those pale green swords thrusting through the earth, soon to be followed by a glorious array of golden daffodils, scarlet tulips and white narcissi. In the words of the poet Shelley:

And the Spring arose on the garden fair,
Like the Spirit of Love felt everywhere;
And each flower and herb on Earth's dark breast
Rose from the dreams of its Wintry rest.

THE FRIENDSHIP BOOK

I HAVE glorified thee on the earth: I have finished the work which thou gavest me to do. And now; O Father, glorify thou me with thine own self with the glory which I had with thee before the world was.

John 17:4-5

A GOOD RETURN

I FELT like spending money,
Not a lot you know,
A little treat that would be nice,
Where should my money go?
Splash out on a smart new dress,
Or tickets for a show?
I decided on some flower seeds —
Now I'll watch my money grow!

Phyllis Ellison.

LIKE most couples, the Lady of the House and I do not always have the same way of doing things and sometimes this can cause a bit of friction.

After one of our little disagreements about how the washing-up should be done, she said to me, "We may not always see eye to eye, Francis, but we can try to see heart to heart."

Seeing each other "heart to heart", I thought, as I pondered her words, is one of the things most needed today — not only at home, but in the whole world.

The Lady of the House isn't always right in what she says, but on this occasion I am sure that she was not wrong.

NOVEMBER

WEDNESDAY—NOVEMBER 1.

WE may be feeling cold today and so I include this poem (author unknown) as a reminder that whatever the weather, He who created the world always has it under his control.

> *Wintry day, frosty day,*
> *God a cloak on all doth lay.*
> *On the earth the snow he sheddeth,*
> *On the sheep the fleece he spreadeth,*
> *Gives the birds a coat of feather*
> *To protect them from the weather.*

THURSDAY—NOVEMBER 2.

OUR old friend Mary likes to keep a stock of pastel-coloured cotton pillowslips and towels by her, and then she spends the Winter months embroidering the flaps with monograms or sprays of flowers in readiness for her special friends or any wedding that comes along.

"Not many people have time for needlework nowadays," says Mary, "but my experience is that they do seem to appreciate an extra touch of hand embroidery."

It's not surprising, I thought, for every stitch of Mary's beautiful work is a labour of love.

"That loving touch" — now, there's a thought . . . Whether it be the care we take in writing a cheerful note to somebody, a bunch of flowers from our own garden or a home-made apple pie for the gentleman living down the road who lives on his own, that extra touch of kindness can make all the difference.

FRIDAY—NOVEMBER 3.

O NE of our young neighbours is a German lady. Each Winter for the last year or two, she has been teaching conversational German at evening classes, and a very competent and confident teacher she is.

However, it hasn't always been like that. She was telling me that she approached the first session with great apprehension, for she knew that all her pupils were older than herself and she wondered how they would relate to her.

"However, I needn't have worried," said Hella, "for a charming elderly couple were sitting in the front row and when they gave me an encouraging smile, it put me at ease right away."

It's surprising what effect the simplest and most unconscious of our acts can have. Even a smile, given at the right time, can help someone more than we might ever imagine.

SATURDAY—NOVEMBER 4.

W ISE words for us to share today from the pen of Henry David Thoreau:
"The most I can do for my friend is simply to be his friend. I have no wealth to bestow on him. If he knows that I am happy in loving him, he will want no other reward. Is not friendship divine in this?"

SUNDAY—NOVEMBER 5.

T HEN the moon shall be confounded, and the sun ashamed, when the Lord of hosts shall reign in mount Zion, and in Jerusalem, and before his ancients gloriously.

Isaiah 24:23

THE FRIENDSHIP BOOK

A MONDAY MORNING PRAYER

IT'S Monday morning again, Lord,
  Another week in view.
Please help me do the best I can
  And walk along with You.
Whatever's round the corner, Lord,
  Just somewhere out of sight,
Help me to meet it cheerfully
  And seek Your guiding light.

The weekend goes so quickly, Lord,
  And Monday's always near.
I think there must be more of them
  All scattered through the year.
Please teach me to be patient, Lord,
  And find the strength I seek.
It's Monday morning yet again . . .
  Go with me through the week!

Iris Hesselden.

I MUST confess to having a weakness for antique fairs. Perhaps, one day, I shall find a treasure when I'm looking at assorted objects of yesteryear — who knows?

Recently I discovered a tiny plate, hardly a collector's item, perhaps, but it pleased me. It cost only a small sum, and has a pretty floral design. The words that go with it are even better:

"All the world's a garden, meant for us to share."

It made me pause and think how lucky we are to see so much beauty around us. How wrong of us not to share what we have.

That plate is my treasure, after all, in its own way!

THE FRIENDSHIP BOOK

I DON'T like being out in fog, but, then, I don't think anyone does. Admittedly, we don't get the "pea soupers" that we used to when most people had coal fires yet even so, when there is freezing fog forecast, I feel alarmed.

On a positive note, one of the things I have noticed is how beautifully the freezing fog picks out a spider's web in the garden. The bad weather has brought about a transformation!

This reminds me of a young neighbour. He lives alone and usually kept himself to himself, until an elderly lady had a nasty fall outside his house. The young man came to her assistance, phoned for an ambulance and accompanied her to hospital. While she was hospitalised, he looked after her little dog, and also kept her garden tidy.

How true it is that people we often don't notice in normal everyday circumstances reveal an unknown and welcome side of their nature when the unexpected happens.

OUT OF PUFF

I DON'T know where the time goes,
There simply isn't enough,
I thought I'd take life easy,
Instead I'm out of puff.
I'm running around in circles,
So many things to do —
If YOU want relaxation,
Then retirement's not for you!

Phyllis Ellison.

L

THE FRIENDSHIP BOOK

*I*T takes two to make a marriage a success, but only
one to make it a failure.

Herbert Louis Samuel.

EVERY November we are urged "Wear Your
Poppy With Pride" in memory of those who died
during the First World War. It was only recently that
I discovered the origin of this custom.

The writer of the verses beginning "In Flanders
fields the poppies blow" was a medical officer with the
First Canadian Army contingent. His poem,
published anonymously in "Punch", was read by an
American lady who was very impressed by the
reference to poppies and thought that the wearing of a
poppy was a highly appropriate way to keep faith with
the fallen.

She wrote "The Victory Emblem" in reply, and
two days before the Armistice in 1918, some of the
overseas war secretaries of the YMCA for whom she
worked gave her a small sum of money with which she
bought two dozen or so red poppies, and sold one to
each of those secretaries. One was a French lady who
suggested that artificial poppies should be made and
sold to help ex-Servicemen and their dependants in
need.

As a result the first-ever Poppy Day was held in
Britain on the third anniversary of the Armistice, at
which time Earl Haig became Founder-President of
the newly-formed British Legion.

Today, 35 million poppies and 65,000 wreaths are
sold to folk who are grateful for the wartime sacrifices
of so many.

M

THE FRIENDSHIP BOOK

NOW thanks be unto God, which always causeth us to triumph in Christ, and maketh manifest the savour of his knowledge by us in every place.

Corinthians II 1:14

MONDAY—NOVEMBER 13.

GARY, aged three, had annoyed his Grandma, and had been soundly told off.

"Oh, dear," said Grandma, as a subdued youngster left the room, "he's taken the huff."

"Gary," shouted his five-year-old brother. "Bring back Grandma's huff at once!"

TUESDAY—NOVEMBER 14.

I WAS reading one of Joyce Grenfell's articles, entitled "My Kind Of Magic". In it she portrayed so beautifully that "what she meant was not the abracadabra kind, but the heightened quality of certain, often quite small experiences lit by unexpected excitement, powerful with innocence." It prompted me to think of what I might have written, given the opportunity.

A new baby must be the most blessed of all kinds of "magic". A tiny fragment of new life, so exquisite and beautiful, entering the world — a miraculous event indeed.

Climbing to the top of a hill and then catching sight of the glorious view; peeping into a bird's nest and seeing lots of tiny wide-open mouths; swimming a first-ever length of a swimming pool; hearing the cuckoo in Spring, or a piece of music special to you.

These are some of my kinds of magic. What are yours?

THE FRIENDSHIP BOOK

ONE minute I was sitting entranced by a delightful travel programme on television — the next, I was in utter darkness. A power cut! There was nothing for it but to start groping in the dark and bumping against the furniture.

It was then, in my own home, that it struck me what being in the dark all the time — being blind — must really mean. Never to see the beauty I had just been watching on the screen; never to look out of the window at a glowing sunset; never to witness the wonder in a child's face.

My first instinct was to make a great resolve — I would seek out and befriend a blind person, I would be their eyes as a thankfulness for my own full sight. Did I find my blind person to help? No, there was no one in the village, so instead I did the next best thing . . . I sent a cheque to the Royal National Institution For The Blind, something I'd never done before.

My resolve was not entirely a failure and that is so often the way in life. If we aim for the stars, maybe we'll only reach the top of the hill to start with, but we're on the way.

CORRIE TEN BOOM wrote these inspiring lines about Him:

> He said, "I long to take your load,
> I want to bear your burdens, too,
> But this you must remember,
> This one thing you must know,
> I cannot take your burden —
> Until you let it go."

THE FRIENDSHIP BOOK

W E have all at some time or other been grateful to a loving aunt," writes a reader from Rustington, and she enclosed these verses:

> *With Mother's Day and Father's Day*
> *And all the dates held dear,*
> *What about an Auntie's Day*
> *To brighten up the year?*
> *Aunties do their share of caring,*
> *Give good advice when sought,*
> *So let's give credit where it's due —*
> *And send a loving thought.*
>
> *What makes aunts so special?*
> *Why, they're loved throughout the land.*
> *Because they make good listeners,*
> *And always understand.*
> *So let's make theirs a special day*
> *Our love and wishes send,*
> *For most importantly of all*
> *Each aunt's a valued friend.*

H AVE you heard this story about the minister who stood up before his congregation one Sunday morning?

"I've got some bad news, some good news and again some more bad news for you. The bad news is that we need £10,000 to repair the church roof; the good news is that we have got the money; the bad news, though, is that it is still in your pockets."

That's certainly a resourceful message!

THE FRIENDSHIP BOOK

FOR by him were all things created, that are in heaven, and that are in earth, visible and invisible, whether they be thrones, or dominions, or principalities, or powers, all things were created by him, and for him.

Colossians 1:16

MONDAY—NOVEMBER 20.

IN a little, ancient church high in a pass of the French Pyrenees there stands a beautiful stone statue of the Madonna. Who carved it and when are a mystery, but if you ask local people, they tell you a strange story . . .

A mountain cowherd had noticed that one of his beasts frequently disappeared for several days. When it returned it always looked stronger and fitter. The next time he saw it set off, he followed until he saw it stop by a lonely pool.

On the way the cowherd had met up with a woodman and now, from their hiding place, they were amazed to see the animal kneel down. Presently the Madonna statue rose out of the water and stood poised before the cow.

The woodman helped the cowherd to carry the statue back with him and it was given pride of place in their church. Countless pilgrims climbed the steep pass to see it and pray at its feet.

Once, robbers stole the Madonna, then fearful of being caught, threw it into a river. Instead of sinking, it rose to the surface, was found and brought back to the church.

Today, pilgrims and tourists still come, though now mostly in cars and coaches, to marvel at the mystery Madonna of the Pyrenees.

THE FRIENDSHIP BOOK

WHEN we visit our friends Joan and Derek we are often amused by the antics of their cat, Thomas. In the sitting-room they have a settee made of leather and there is nothing that Thomas likes better than his seat on the slippery back of the settee. The only trouble is that when he becomes relaxed and falls asleep, he often slides off on to the floor!

"You never learn, Thomas, do you?" laughs Joan as, nothing daunted, he jumps back on to his perch.

I could quite understand Joan's remark, for I am a great believer in learning from mistakes; yet I can't help admiring that cat for his persistence. At present he hasn't solved the problem but I feel sure that one day he will. After all, there aren't many things that can't be accomplished through perseverance!

I WOULD like to pass on to you an extract from a letter that I have received from a friend. Some months previously, Joan's husband had died very suddenly, and she had been left completely alone. Life was never to be the same again. Here is what she now writes:

"The world had been full of sunshine, every moment filled with joy. I never dreamed that it all could end so suddenly and that loneliness would blight my life.

"Well, I've now spent many hours in grief and pain, but I realise that I must look past the clouds and search for the sunshine again. New hope must rise from the ashes of the past, then through this new awakening I will find joy again."

I hope others in trouble will find fresh hope from Joan's brave words.

THE FRIENDSHIP BOOK

HAVE you heard about the picture "Opportunity"? It depicts a lady with a lot of hair at the front, but none at all at the back. The moral of the painting is that we should grasp "Opportunity" as she approaches us, for if we fail to do so, then she has gone for ever, because there is nothing to hold on to when she has passed by.

Shakespeare put it this way: "There is a tide in the affairs of men, which, taken at the flood, leads on to fortune" — whilst Lord Reith of the BBC said, "I do not like crises, but I do like the opportunities they provide."

More recently, and on the same theme, the politician Shirley Williams said, "There are hazards in anything one does, but there are greater hazards in doing nothing."

THE BIG DECISION

"I'M not going to school today,"
Was the claim of little Jack.
"It's all an awful waste of time,
So I'm never going back."

"Teacher keeps on asking questions,
And I'm sure as sure can be,
That she does not know the answers,
'Cos she keeps on asking me."

After sitting, deep in thought,
Jack jumped up in glee,
"I think I'd better go to school,
For that teacher might need me."

Elizabeth Shankland.

SATURDAY—NOVEMBER 25.

IF you have ever noticed a dog with an orange-coloured collar and lead and thought it might have special significance, then you would be correct, for the dog would be registered with the charity "Hearing Dogs For The Deaf". The scheme began in order to help people suffering from the totally invisible handicap of deafness.

Like "Guide Dogs For The Blind", Hearing Dogs undergo rigorous selection and training, but whereas dogs for blind people are nearly always Alsatians or Labradors, those trained for deaf people are mostly mongrels from animal rescue centres.

The advantage of this is that they are more inclined to use their initiative than pedigree dogs and this is very important when the dog needs to distinguish between a routine, everyday sound and one that its owner's attention needs to be drawn to immediately — such as the telephone, a knock at the door or a potentially dangerous situation.

Once a dog has been trained and placed with its new owner, it is on trial for three months and during this time members of the training centre are in frequent contact, giving support and ironing out any problems that may arise.

Dogs may be entrusted to a young person deaf from birth or to someone older who has recently become deaf. When that person lives alone then their Hearing Dog is not only a loved and valued companion, but their ears and security as well.

SUNDAY—NOVEMBER 26.

FOR thou art my lamp, O Lord; and the Lord will lighten my darkness.

Samuel II 22:29

THE PERFECT CASTLE

THE FRIENDSHIP BOOK

I CALLED round one day to see one of our elderly neighbours who is often housebound during the Winter months. He was just in the middle of watching his favourite soap opera so I joined him in a cup of tea and watched the remainder of it with him.

As he turned off the television, he said, "I hope you didn't mind me watching this, but when you live alone these people become your friends."

I could understand what he meant. Television is a boon when we are not able to get out and about and most of us have favourite programmes which we watch regularly. However, let's try to make sure that there is no lonely person living in our street who is solely dependent for company on the images of a television screen. There's no substitute for regular personal contact with those close to us.

HOW many people do you know who are pessimists? They are the ones who always look on the gloomy side of life.

Fortunately, most of our friends do not fit that description, but sadly, there are many in this world who do. For them, when a small cloud passes over a Summer sky it heralds a thunderstorm. If they sneeze, it is a sure sign of a cold coming. A partly-used bottle is always half-empty, never half-full!

Pessimists are the folk who say, "What have I to smile about? The cost of living has gone up again!"

That kind of negative attitude clouds the enjoyment of life. There is a verse in the book of Proverbs that sums it up:

"A merry heart doeth good like a medicine, but a broken spirit drieth the bones."

THE FRIENDSHIP BOOK

IT had been a frustrating church council meeting. The young minister in charge had plenty of good new ideas, but they were criticised and voted down by one particular member whose daughter was to go into hospital for an operation.

When the meeting was over, the minister said to his critic, "How are you travelling to see Jane when she goes into hospital?"

"Oh, I'll be going by bus," came the reply.

"Oh, there's no need for that," declared the young man. "I'll drive you."

Over 20 years later, that act of kindness is still remembered by someone who is honest enough to admit that if she had been on the receiving end of such criticism that evening, *she* certainly wouldn't have put herself out to help her critic!

FAMILY MEETINGS

FAMILY meetings, so much pleasure
So many memories to treasure,
Remembering our childhood days
Happy hours, and carefree ways.

Chatting and exchanging news
Sometimes airing all our views,
But if there's friction, make amends
Be sure that all depart as friends.

For future years may bring regret
If quarrels linger on — and yet
What greater asset can there be
Than a loving family.

Dorothy M. Loughran.

DECEMBER

FRIDAY—DECEMBER 1.

IT was one of those dark, cloudy Winter days. A friend we met on our way home said, "Never mind, Spring is only a snowdrop away now."

Strangely, that same evening I found this little piece written about the snowdrop:

> *Its frailty tells of His might and power,*
> *Its whiteness of His infinite purity,*
> *Its delicate green of life given by Him,*
> *The multitudes of them tell of his generosity,*
> *Its delicate structure calls forth awe and wonder.*

These are beautiful thoughts about the tiny flower that never ceases to bloom, even in the coldest of weather. Who but Someone Infinite could have created anything so exquisite?

SATURDAY—DECEMBER 2.

CHILDREN have a great talent for providing explanations when adults are baffled. Two sisters were once looking at a book of religious pictures and came across a scene showing the Virgin Mary and Baby Jesus.

"See," said the elder, "that's Jesus and that's his mother."

"But where is his father?" the younger one wanted to know. Her sister thought for a moment then came up with a bright idea. "Oh, he must be taking the picture, of course!"

Good thinking!

THE FRIENDSHIP BOOK

FOR there is one God, and one mediator between God and men, the man Christ Jesus.

Timothy I 2:5

WHENEVER I go to church at Christmas and stand before the Nativity tableau of the stable, the Holy Family and the shepherds, I remember the story of the boy who wanted a wheelbarrow for Christmas.

Many years ago when the Dean went into his cathedral to check that all was well, he noticed a small boy in ragged clothing kneeling in front of the crib and praying, "Please can I have a wheelbarrow for Christmas?"

When he made enquiries about the boy, he found that young though he was, he was the man of the house and he badly needed the wheelbarrow to collect wood to keep the fire going for his mother in their poor home.

The Dean called together some of the congregation and told them of the boy's prayer. Between them they produced a sturdy wheelbarrow, filled it with Christmas fare and warm clothing for the family, and left it outside the boy's door on Christmas Eve.

Early next morning the Dean was in the cathedral when in came the boy, scrubbed and tidy and pushing the empty wheelbarrow. When he reached the crib he stopped, gently picked up the doll representing Jesus, placed it in his wheelbarrow and wheeled it round the cathedral.

"And what are you doing?" asked the Dean.

"Well, sir," said the boy, "I asked Him for it. It's only right that He should have the first ride."

THE FRIENDSHIP BOOK

DID you know that television has its patron saint? She was St Clare who lived from 1194 to 1253. The legend is that she was too ill to go to church, yet she knew what was happening there because she had a vision which enabled her to see the whole service in detail.

I sometimes think of her as I watch television, or hear people talking about their favourite programmes. I think of her, too, when I hear the phrase sometimes heard in broadcasting: "Please do not adjust your set. Some viewers may be experiencing interference." I wonder if it is St Clare busy because she does not like what's been shown!

Seriously, television does deserve a patron saint. I like to think of St Clare watching over the dedicated people behind the programmes — the writers, editors, presenters, actors, engineers and camera crews who do their best to keep us entertained and informed.

OUR friend Mary has been kept indoors with a chesty cold, so the Lady of the House and I called round with a few groceries and asked if there were any little jobs that needed doing, despite the fact that Mary's little house looked as neat and shiny as it always does.

"Well, Francis," explained Mary, "it hasn't been easy, but I do like to keep things nice. If I wake up one morning and tell myself 'I can't do the dusting today', then tomorrow I might say, 'I won't do the dusting today' and then the day might come when I don't do any dusting at all — and where would I be then?"

With a philosophy like that, I'm sure there won't be much that will defeat Mary!

THE FRIENDSHIP BOOK

IN a little book of religious poems by Marion Elliott, I came on these four moving verses:

> *I dreamt of a world without sorrow,*
> *I dreamt of a world without hate,*
> *I dreamt of a world of rejoicing,*
> *And I woke to find Christ at my gate.*

> *I dreamt of a world without hunger,*
> *I dreamt of a world without war,*
> *I dreamt of a world full of loving,*
> *And I woke to find Christ at my door.*

> *I dreamt of a world without anger,*
> *I dreamt of a world without pride,*
> *I dreamt of a world of compassion,*
> *And I woke to find Christ at my side.*

> *I dreamt of this world of tomorrow,*
> *I dreamt of this world set apart,*
> *I dreamt of this world full of glory,*
> *And I woke to find Christ in my heart.*

HERE is a story from South Africa. A little Afrikaans boy was asked to take part in a Nativity play. He was told to be the innkeeper, and that when Mary and Joseph arrived, he would have to say, "There is no room at the inn."

He was horrified at being asked to do this, but he took the part and when the time came he said, "There is no room at the inn — *maar kom binne vir 'n dop.*" (but come in for a drink!)

THE MASTER'S TOUCH

THE FRIENDSHIP BOOK

"A GOOD marriage is like a typewriter. The spools are the husband and wife, working in smooth harmony, and the ribbon is the love that flows between them."

Maurice Fleming.

HIS name shall endure for ever: his name shall be continued as long as the sun; and men shall be blessed in him; all nations shall call him blessed.

Psalms 72:17

ONE Christmas, a few friends and neighbours came round for a mince pie and coffee, and, through our introduction, two of them struck up a friendship that was to last for a long time.

It was a great joy to watch this relationship start and flourish, especially when some years later, in retirement, both were victims of what they called "Arthur-itis". One thought that this was only to be expected, and so accepted it, but the other said he would call on another friend, "Will Power", to help him fight it.

Because of their different attitudes, they were able to help and influence each other in their time of need. They also gave each other practical help when they could, as well as words of encouragement when needed. It was indeed a blessing for both that they had become such friends all these years previously.

Samuel Johnson once said: "If a man does not make new acquaintances as he advances through life, he will soon find himself left alone."

THE FRIENDSHIP BOOK

IT always does me good to read about a little lady who lived with her brother in a cottage at Grasmere in the heart of the Lake District.

She looked after his every need, and without any modern conveniences she would bake, keep house, and provide hospitality for his friends and the important people who visited him. They all went away, not thinking of the poet William Wordsworth but of his quiet, loving and intelligent sister, Dorothy. When I read her journal, it always teaches me a lesson or two.

Despite all the hard work she did at Dove Cottage, she also found time to help the poor of the district and they grew to love her for her concern and gentleness as much as her generosity.

I would like to have met Dorothy Wordsworth.

A SEASONAL VIEW

FROST on the dark cones of the fir,
Frost on the holly bough,
Gather the yew and mistletoe,
Gather the ivy, now!
Bright are the berries, scarlet red,
Bright as the robin's breast.
Hark to the sound of carols sung,
Hark to the Yuletide blessed!
Watch to the midnight, chiming hour,
Watch for the dawn to bring
Christmas, to herald peace on earth —
Christmas, for our Christ-born King!

Elizabeth Gozney.

THE FRIENDSHIP BOOK

THE members of a church I heard about liked to exchange Christmas cards with one another. It became such a widespread custom that each December a specially-constructed board, with ledges, was placed at the back of the church, so that people could "post" their cards alphabetically, picking up the ones that had been left for themselves. Great numbers of cards exchanged hands.

Then, one year, members of the ladies' fellowship decided that instead of giving cards to the friends they saw each week in church, they would give the money earmarked for cards to a charity instead. They heard that a warehouse had been made available in London, and Christmas fare was to be provided for some of the city's homeless. This, they decided, was where their money should go.

After Christmas they received a letter of thanks from the organisers, describing events and informing the group that their contribution had been sufficient to provide turkey for the Christmas guests.

Those who had helped to provide the meal were pleased to know exactly what their gift had been spent on and are eager to participate in future. I wouldn't be at all surprised, now that they know about it, if many more people in that church decide to spread a bit of good cheer in the years to come.

I COULDN'T help chuckling at the story I heard about the teenage lads who were standing on the corner opposite a church one Sunday evening in December.

One was heard to say, "I don't know who this Carol Service is, but she certainly packs them in . . ."

SATURDAY—DECEMBER 16.

THE Lady Of The House had been given a new "My Recipe" book as a not-quite-Christmas present, and one afternoon she busied herself transferring tried and tested favourites from a rather shabby and finger-smudged old scrapbook to the replacement.

"Oh, look, Francis!" she exclaimed. "Do you remember Mrs Brown who gave me this recipe for those mouth-watering chocolate slices you love? She was a dear soul, wasn't she, always helping others, I remember. What about old Joe who lived next door? Here's his steak and kidney pudding recipe — I remember how he was always giving away his allotment produce."

So, as each recipe was neatly copied out, we were reminded of kind folk who'd been part of our lives and whose influence was still being remembered. Their recipes were not only for good food, but also recipes for life.

SUNDAY—DECEMBER 17.

AND the angel answered and said unto her, The Holy Ghost shall come upon thee, and the power of the Highest shall overshadow thee: therefore also that holy thing which shall be born of thee shall be called the Son of God.

Luke 1:35

MONDAY—DECEMBER 18.

WE have all said things we regretted. I often recall the warning given by an American poet, Carl Sandburg:

"Look out how you use proud words. When you let proud words go, it is not easy to call them back."

DEEP DECEMBER

TUESDAY—DECEMBER 19.

DO miracles happen? Mr T. J. Kavanagh of Edinburgh believes they do.

"In December 1921 I was in France on business and found myself at St Omer with some time to spare.

"Remembering that an old boyhood friend, William Martin Brand of the Argyll and Sutherland Highlanders, had been killed near St Omer in 1917, I decided to try to find his grave. I made enquiries and learned that the British Military Cemetery was at Longueresse about 1½ miles away. I set off on foot, but when I arrived, daylight was almost gone and the cemetery gates were closed.

"A woman in a café told me I could get into the cemetery over the low wall at the back. Armed with a box of matches, I began to examine the graves, but soon realised that the task was impossible, not only because of the large number of graves, but also because of the difficulty in reading the names on the wooden crosses. I went back to the café and explained that I would have to give up, but she told me she would give me a candle and that her young daughter would hold it for me.

"We searched for some time until I told the girl we would have to give up. However, on the way back, she suddenly stopped and said, 'Will you not try again?' To please her, I took the candle and held it to the cross where she was standing — it was my friend's grave.

"Was that a coincidence, or did God inspire the little girl to stop and to ask, 'Will you not try again?' "

WEDNESDAY—DECEMBER 20.

THESE words of Benjamin Franklin were quoted to me by an American friend:

"Be slow in choosing a friend, slower in changing."

WITH THANKS!

WE pray to God in times of stress,
But when in realms of happiness,
Do we find time to stop, and say —
"Thank you, God, for a perfect day"?

Elizabeth Gozney.

FRIDAY—DECEMBER 22.

TO be 70 years young is sometimes far more cheerful and hopeful than to be 40 years old.

Oliver Wendell Holmes.

SATURDAY—DECEMBER 23.

LITTLE James Walker was born a beautiful, golden-haired baby, the apple of his mother's eye. However, when he was three it was discovered that he would always have the mental age of a two-year-old. Once the traumatic news was accepted by his family and friends, life continued as usual for the Walkers.

James is now 12. He attends a special school for most of the time, so we don't see a lot of this cheery lad, except during the holidays.

You can imagine how pleased I was last Christmas, to hear carol singers coming up the lane. As I peered out at the young, and not so young faces, their hot breath steaming in the biting cold of the December evening, my pleasure was heightened when among them I saw young James.

How nice today that people have learned not only to accept those less fortunate than themselves, but are encouraging them to participate in everyday activities.

SUNDAY—DECEMBER 24.

AND when they were come into the house, they saw the young child with Mary his mother, and fell down, and worshipped him: and when they had opened their treasures, they presented unto him gifts; gold, and frankincense, and myrrh.

Matthew 2:11

MONDAY—DECEMBER 25.

OUR friend Emily loves poetry and often copies pieces that particularly appeal to her into her notebook of treasures. This one by Laurence Housman is, I think, one of the loveliest of Christmas poems:

Light looked down and beheld Darkness,
"Thither will I go," said Light.
Peace looked down and beheld War,
"Thither will I go," said Peace.
Love looked down and beheld Hatred,
"Thither will I go," said Love.
So came Light, and shone;
So came Peace, and gave rest;
So came Love, and brought Life,
And the Word was made Flesh, and dwelt among us.

TUESDAY—DECEMBER 26.

WILLIE'S Sunday School teacher asked him, "If you had a large, good apple and a small, wormy one, and you were told to divide them with your brother, which would you give him?" Quick as lightning came the reply, "Do you mean my big brother or my little one?"

I can see that it might make a difference!

THE FRIENDSHIP BOOK

DO you enjoy listening to request programmes on the radio? Sometimes, if I'm in the kitchen while the Lady of the House is busy dusting or vacuuming, I hear snatches of the dedications of a special tune for a birthday, a wedding anniversary, or perhaps to cheer up a patient in hospital.

One day a lady had written to say that because of poor health she was unable to travel to sunny parts for a holiday. However, when a friend came to spend a few days with her, she felt she had done just that because it was "like walking in the sunshine".

It's a lovely thought, and one that I pass on to you today. What may seem a very small thing to us can bring immense pleasure to a housebound or lonely person. Let's do all we can to help somebody else to "take a walk in the sunshine".

HAVE you ever stopped to wonder how some of our most-used phrases originated? The one I am particularly thinking of is when we speak of seeing something through to the bitter end.

The expression goes back 400 years to the days of sailing ships. The strong posts on the deck of a ship for securing ropes were called bitts. When the ropes had been paid out to the bitter end, that was as far as they could go. In modern ships these posts are still called bitts.

Nowadays, when we talk about "seeing things through to the bitter end", we are referring to a situation that may be difficult, unpleasant or even dangerous, but which with perseverance, determination and courage we can see through to a satisfactory conclusion.

FRIDAY—DECEMBER 29.

BEFORE you settle down to sleep tonight, take heed of these wise words:

"If an apple a day keeps the doctor away, a prayer a night keeps the Devil from sight."

SATURDAY—DECEMBER 30.

FIRST-FOOTING is a well-known New Year tradition, especially in Scotland. It's a lovely custom when family and friends gather together to see in the New Year, waiting eagerly for the knock on the door heralding the arrival of the first foot. To bring the greatest luck to the household, he should be tall and dark, but no-one worries if he isn't.

Nearly everyone keeps open house on Hogmanay, ready to welcome relations, neighbours, friends. Petty differences are forgotten and there is a feeling of warmth and friendship.

Wouldn't it be marvellous if we could keep up this warmth all through the year? We make such a tremendous effort for this one night: how splendid it would be if we could spend just ten or fifteen minutes regularly each month, in the service of others.

Perhaps we could call on the lonely or the housebound folk to ask how they're keeping — just a brief visit and a few words to show we care. I'm sure you can think of others in the community who deserve extra thought. It would help to keep that warm feeling of friendship and goodwill alive so much longer, wouldn't it?

SUNDAY—DECEMBER 31.

I AM the door: by me if any man enter in, he shall be saved, and shall go in and out, and find pasture.

John 10:9

Where The Photographs Were Taken

FOLLOW ME — *River Dove, Derbyshire.*
CRISP AND EVEN — *Woodmancote, Gloucestershire.*
GRACE — *The River Cherwell.*
WATER COLOURS — *Lulworth Cove, Dorset.*
BRIGHT AND BEAUTIFUL — *Thakeham Church, West Sussex.*
ABBEY BLOSSOM TIME — *Milton Abbey, Dorset.*
WHO NEEDS A BRIDGE? — *River Lyd, Dartmoor.*
SPRING DELIGHT — *Chalkney Wood, Earls Colne, Essex.*
COUNTRY CALM — *Thaxted, Essex.*
HOW GREEN IS MY VALLEY — *Bedd Gelert, Gwynedd.*
CLUBBING TOGETHER — *Helen's Bay, County Down.*
PROUD PARENTS — *River Avon, Malmesbury.*
BLUE HEAVEN — *Rosemullion Head, Cornwall.*
MONARCHS OF THE GLEN — *Glen Coe.*
SUMMER COOL — *River Barle, Exmoor.*
GUARDIAN OF THE NIGHT — *Mount Orgueil Castle, Jersey.*
REFLECTING — *River Wye, Monsal Dale.*
SMALL IS BEAUTIFUL — *Babbacombe, Devon.*
STILL SUMMER — *Brill, Oxfordshire.*
JUST CHATTING — *Knaresborough Castle, Yorkshire.*
REST AND BE THANKFUL — *Ashness Bridge, Derwentwater.*
THE PERFECT CASTLE — *Eilean Donan, Ross and Cromarty.*
DEEP DECEMBER — *Bourton on the Water, Gloucestershire.*

ACKNOWLEDGEMENTS: **David Askham;** Rest and Be Thankful. **Ivan Belcher;** Follow Me, Reflecting, Small Is Beautiful. **Paul Felix;** Crisp And Even, Proud Parents, Still Summer, The Master's Touch, Deep December. **V.K. Guy;** Two Happy People, Grace, The Perfect Castle. **V.B. Hicks;** Who Needs A Bridge?, Golden Wonder. **Dennis Mansell;** Spring Delight, Blue Heaven. **Picturepoint;** Woodland Wonder, How Green Is My Valley, Buttercup Meadow. **Clifford Robinson;** Summer Cool, Just Chatting, Facing 17th Sept. **Kenneth Scowen;** Bright And Beautiful, Abbey Blossom Time. **Andy Williams;** Water Colours, Country Calm, Clubbing Together, Monarchs Of The Glen, Guardian Of The Night, Facing 24th Dec.

Printed and Published by D. C. THOMSON & CO., LTD.,
185 Fleet Street, London EC4A 2HS.
© D. C. THOMSON & Co., Ltd., 1994

ISBN 0-85116-588-5